Developmental Childrearing:

For Parents of Children Ages Five to Ten

by

Libby R. Hoffman

Copyright ©1983
EDUCATIONAL MEDIA CORPORATION®
P. O. Box 21311
Minneapolis, Minneota 55421

Library of Congress Catalog Card No. 83-080005
ISBN 0-932796-14-1

Leader's Guide—

Library of Congress Catalog Card No. 83-080005
ISBN 0-932796-15-X

Printing (Last Digit)

9 8 7 6 5 4 3 2 1

No part of this book may be reproduced or used in any form without the expressed permission of the publisher in writing. Manufactured in the United States of America.

Production editor —

Don L. Sorenson

Graphic design —

Earl Sorenson

Illustrations —

Mary M. McKee

Dedication

To Jim, Andi and Debbie who helped so much

Table of Contents

Introduction   1

The First Meeting   9

   Background   9
   Orientation to the Parent Group Program   10
   Members' Role and Responsibilities in the Program   11
   Purpose and Format of the Program   12
   Study Phase   13
      Gesell's Theory of Child Development;
      Stages of Five and Six Year Olds
   Homework Assignment   17
   Counseling Phase   18

The Second Meeting   19

   Study Phase   20
      Gesell's Theory: Stages of Seven through
      Ten Year Olds; Children's Needs
      and Childrearing Approaches
   Homework Assignment   34
   Counseling Phase   34

The Third Meeting   37

   Study Phase   37
      Erikson's Theory of Psychosocial Development;
      Childrearing Approaches
   Homework Assignment   47
   Counseling Phase   48

The Fourth Meeting   49

   Study Phase   49
      Adlerian Theory of Personality Development;
      Children's Goals and Behavior; The Role of Family
      and Home Life; Birth Order
   Homework Assignment   60
   Counseling Phase   60

The Fifth Meeting 61

Study Phase 61
Mistaken Goals of Misbehavior; Adlerian Childrearing Approaches; Practice Exercise—Mistaken Goals
Homework Assignment 83
Counseling Phase 84

The Sixth Meeting 85

Study Phase 85
The Use of Natural and Logical Consequences as Methods of Discipline; Listening Techniques Practice Exercise—Identifying Feelings of Children
Homework Assignment 93
Counseling Phase 94

The Seventh Meeting 95

Study Phase 95
Responding to Children's Feelings; Practice Exercise—Parents' Self-Statements
Homework Assignment 103
Counseling Phase 104

The Eighth Meeting 105

Study Phase 105
Family Problem Solving; Summary of Childrearing Practices
Counseling Phase 112

A Message to Parents 113

References 119

About the Author

Libby R. Hoffman is a licensed professional counselor who specializes in counseling with children and parents. She also is Supervisor for Elementary and Middle School Guidance for the Virginia Department of Education. Previously, she has been an adjunct professor at Virginia Commonwealth University and an elementary school counselor and teacher.

Dr. Hoffman is the author or co-author of a variety of articles and training materials in the field of counseling and group work. She has been active in state and national professional associations over the past ten years and has conducted numerous workshops about group work with parents.

She holds an Ed.D. in counseling from the University of Virginia, and an M.Ed. in counselor education from Virginia Commonwealth University, She also has completed post-masters degree work at the College of William and Mary. Dr. Hoffman attended the University of Michigan and received a B.S. in early childhood education from Syracuse University.

Introduction

Parenthood is one of the most significant roles we assume during our lifetime. Although children are affected by siblings, peers, and adults other than parents, the key persons in their lives during the childhood years are their parents.

Children are deeply influenced by what parents say and do as well as by what they fail to say and do. The kind of person a child becomes is determined to a great extent by the nature and quality of childrearing during the period from birth to ten years of age.

The childrearing methods parents employ during these formative years are of critical importance to children's development. They have enormous impact upon the self concepts, attitudes, beliefs, feelings, values, confidence, and modes of behavior children form. Through their interactions with parents, children arrive at lasting conclusions about themselves, others, and their world. These become the very foundations of personality.

Despite the significance of the parenting role, most parents recieve little or no formal preparation or training to help them to be effective childrearers. It seems ironic that training is required in our society for many professional and occupational roles, while parents are expected to be competent in raising children without any formal preparation.

Largely due to the lack of training, parents, unaware of the harmful effects, may use damaging childrearing methods which have been employed for countless generations. Parents tend to rear children in much the same way as they were raised. Thus, such negative practices as severe autocratic disciplining, humiliation and shame, overprotection, and excessive restrictiveness continue to be used in the belief that they are helpful to children.

Much valuable information has resulted from research about child development and childrearing methods which can be used to benefit children and parents. It is time to cast aside the myth that parents are somehow magically endowed with the abilities to rear children well because of the love they have for them. Love alone is not enough. Constructive childrearing requires that parents also have knowledge and skills. The most effective way for parents to acquire the essential knowledge and skills is by participation in parent education programs.

In recent years, parents and professionals who work with children and families have become increasingly aware of the need for parent education programs. Regardless of such factors as years of education, socioeconomic background, the number of children, and whether or not both parents reside in the home, parents are likely to experience concerns and difficulties as their children move through the various stages of development.

Parent concerns usually are related to such childrearing areas as methods of discipline; fostering responsibility in children; school performance and adjustment; parent-child relations; children's relationships with siblings and peers; adjustment problems resulting from divorce, death, or illness; negative attitudes and behaviors; sex education; and moral development.

Some parents encounter continued difficulties in one or more of these areas throughout the childrearing years. Others experience problems primarily when their children are going through particularly difficult and trying stages of development. The stress and anxiety resulting from these difficulties tend to be detrimental to the well-being of children and parents and damaging to harmonious family life.

Many parents try to cope alone with their childrearing problems rather than by turning to others for help. When they do seek assistance, it is likely to be from friends, family members, teachers, or pediatricians after problems have become severe. Frequently, the solutions offered by these people are inadequate for resolving the immediate difficulties. Rarely does this crisis-oriented approach provide parents with the knowledge, understandings, and skills for dealing effectively with future childrearing concerns.

In response to the need for parent education, a wide variety of "self-help" books, articles, television programs, films, and lectures about childrearing have appeared on the scene in the past several years. Their popularity is strong evidence that parents desire to improve the quality of their childrearing.

While these approaches are of some value, it is important to recognize their limitations in providing lasting benefits. Although they do furnish information to parents about child development and parenting techniques, they generally offer no opportunity for parents to engage in activities to help them apply the new learning to their individual childrearing concerns.

To provide meaningful and lasting benefits, parent training must consist of more than just facts. It also must provide parents with the opportunity to participate over a period of time with other parents in a systematic program of learning experiences under the guidance of a trained group leader. These experiences must be designed to assist parents in the following:

  1. To better understand children, their development, goals, and behaviors.

2. To gain greater insight and understanding about ourselves as parents and to develop more positive childrearing attitudes and behaviors.
3. To relate information about child development and constructive childrearing techniques to our own particular childrearing concerns and difficulties.
4. To practice and polish skills in utilizing constructive childrearing techniques.
5. To employ newly acquired insights, knowledge, and skills for providing more constructive childrearing for children.

In summary, effective parent education — parent training that will make a positive difference in the lives of children and parents — requires both an informational component and one that provides for experiential learning in a group setting with the assistance of a professional group leader.

In light of this, the *Developmental Childrearing* (DC) program was created and field tested. It was designed to be used with parents of children ages five through ten by counselors, psychologists, social workers, and other professionals trained in child development and group work. This comprehensive program features the study of child development and childrearing techniques along with group counseling experiences for individual parent growth, problem solving, and decision making. Its goals are: 1) to help parents acquire the information, understandings, attitudes, skills, and abilities essential for effective parenting; and 2) to furnish encouragement and support to help them provide quality childrearing.

Developmental Childrearing is composed of eight two-hour group meetings, each of which consists of two phases. The first 45-minute phase of each meeting focuses upon the study of children's developmental stages, needs, and typical modes of behavior, and upon constructive childrearing practices. These study phases contain information from the work of a number of child development specialists and psychologists.

Attention is devoted to the cycles of behavioral development in children, according to Arnold Gesell (Ilg and Ames, 1955). Erik Erikson's theory of the psychosocial stages of development is included to promote additional understanding of the developmental stages, needs, and tasks of childhood (Erikson, 1963). It is hoped that this understanding will enable parents to meet more effectively children's developmental needs and to cope more confidently with the many dilemmas encountered in childrearing.

Based upon the theory of Alfred Adler and the writings of Dreikurs and Stoltz (1964), study segments are provided to increase parents' knowledge of personality development and childrearing approaches which encourage self-discipline and responsibility in children. Also presented are communication techniques used by counseling professionals and described in the work of Thomas Gordon (1975). These techniques help parents to interact with children in ways which foster positive parent-child relations. Information regarding the characteristics of effective parents, as described by Burton White and Jean Watts (1973), is included to provide further insight about the childrearing methods suggested in the program.

In addition to group study and discussion, other activities such as practice exercises and role playing are employed during some of the study phases. These are important for assisting parents to internalize the information presented and to become skillful in using the recommended childrearing methods. Because of the broad scope of information included in the program, it is strongly advised that parents take time to study and review the materials outside the sessions and also complete the homework suggested.

Following the study phase of each session, a 15-minute coffee break is recommended. During this break, parents have the opportunity for relaxation and informal conversation with each other.

The second hour of each session is devoted to parent group counseling to promote personal parent growth and individual problem solving related to childrearing. Group counseling is a most effective approach for helping parents to understand themselves — their feelings, attitudes, motives, values, and behaviors in parent-child relations. It also provides a supportive setting in which to make necessary decisions and constructive changes regarding childrearing.

Certain factors are of vital importance in order for there to be positive outcomes for parents from the group counseling experience. First, it is essential that parents participating in the group feel a real sense of commitment to receive help with their childrearing concerns from the group. Along with this, they must understand that they also have the responsibility to try to help the other members to deal with their concerns and difficulties related to raising children.

The second factor has to do with confidentiality. Members must be willing to keep in strict confidence what other parents in the group reveal about themselves and their personal concerns. This means that members may not discuss outside the counseling group other members' concerns or behaviors. More detailed explanations of the group counseling process and the roles and responsibilities of the members are provided later as each of the eight parent meetings is described.

Developmental Childrearing was first used in 1978-1979 in a study involving ten groups of parents of elementary school children in a large urban setting. The findings of the study revealed several important outcomes. Participation in the program significantly increased the parents' ability to recognize the goals of children's behavior and enabled them to know how to respond in a more constructive manner to their children. It also made a significant positive difference in their attitudes of understanding; that is, mutual parent-child sharing of ideas, feelings, and attitudes. Furthermore, parents showed large gains in their ability to interpret their children's behavior and understand their own roles in influencing that behavior.

At the completion of the study, reactions to *Developmental Childrearing* from the counselors who conducted the groups and from the parents who received the training were highly favorable. The counselors, all of whom had previous experience in conducting parent education groups, viewed it as an extremely effective vehicle for use in parent training. They approved of the program's format and content and felt that it was more effective than previous types of approaches which they had employed. Furthermore, they reported many observable benefits from the program in terms of increased parent understanding of childrearing and improved attitudes and skills.

Parent reactions to the program also were very positive. Some of their comments are as follows:

- "Communication with my child has improved."
- "I am more consistent."
- "I now realize that discipline develops a sense of security in children."
- "My expectations of my children have increased."
- "I holler less."

- "I now avoid repeating myself and avoid power struggles."
- "I feel I have more self-control in my relationships with my children."
- "I spank less."
- "I listen more."
- "My kids are calmer and more affectionate."
- "My husband has read the material and we are both trying the same approaches."
- "I am now using punishment (effective forms of discipline) for the first time and feel less guilty about it."
- "I learned a lot about myself."
- "It's a comfort knowing that other parents have similar problems."

In essence, the parents and counselors felt that *Developmental Childrearing* is worthwhile, effective, and needed by parents. Since that original study, the program has continued to be used with groups of parents in that same city and in other geographical areas, both rural and urban. Where feedback regarding these subsequent groups has been provided to the author, benefits for parents and children continue to be reported.

It is important to note again that this is a program designed for use with parents in groups. Although much valuable information about children and childrearing is provided in the study phases of the meetings, parent involvement and participation in the group counseling and group activities are key elements in determining positive outcomes.

The First Meeting

Background

The initial meeting of the parent group is important in setting the direction and climate for future meetings. Therefore, a period of time at the beginning of this session is devoted to getting acquainted; describing members' roles and responsibilities in the program; and defining the goals and format of the program. Because of these special activities, the time allocated during this meeting for the study phase is only 15 minutes rather than the usual 45 minutes.

Most parents tend to feel somewhat apprehensive and uneasy at the beginning of this first session. This is a normal reaction when we find ourselves in a new and different situation and are not certain about how well things will go for us. Parents may help themselves to relax and enjoy more fully the first meeting by remembering that such reactions are typical and that the others present are experiencing similar feelings. The group leader is aware that most members are likely to be feeling ill at ease and will make every effort to help each person present feel welcome and an important member of the group.

Each member brings to the parent group one's own unique personality, abilities, values, beliefs, experiences, and concerns.

As we participate in the program, we soon discover that, despite these differences, we share many similar feelings, experiences, problems, and concerns about childrearing. Both our uniqueness and our similarities will contribute to making the parent group experience productive and beneficial.

The following sections describe the format, activities, and content of the first meeting. Included in the section entitled *Study Phase One* is an explanation and description of children's typical behaviors for ages five and six according to the child studies of Arnold Gesell. These have been adapted from *Child Behavior from Birth to Ten* (Ilg and Ames, 1955).

Orientation to the Parent Group Program

Welcoming remarks. The group leader will provide a brief introduction to the program and a review of the schedule for group meetings.

Get-Acquainted Activity. (20 Minutes) This short exercise is intended to be an ice-breaker. One of the two following activities will be used as a means for helping the group members to become acquainted and to feel more comfortable in this new setting. At the discretion of the group leader, an alternative approach may be selected for this purpose.

Activity 1. Parents select partners and interview their partners for a period of five minutes, a total of ten minutes for each pair. The total group then reconvenes and the members introduce their individual partners to the group. At the conclusion of these introductions, the leader summarizes by pointing out similarities disclosed regarding parents' interests, concerns, likes, dislikes, and so forth.

Activity 2. Large newsprint and crayons or magic markers are distributed to each member. Each participant draws a picture describing self; i.e., interests, hobbies, likes, dislikes, and so forth. Then members introduce themselves using the drawings as aids. During this process, the leader encourages interaction among the members. In summary, at the conclusion of the activity, the leader points out the similarities of interests and concerns expressed by the members.

Group Discussion of Members' Role and Responsibilities in the Program

(Discussion time: 5 minutes)

Because *Developmental Childrearing* is a group program, responsibility for the successful functioning of the group is shared jointly by the parent group members and the group leader. Therefore, it is important that the roles and responsibilities of the members of the group be clearly understood.

During the following discussion, it is suggested that parents consider each of the items presented in terms of their own personal feelings and willingness to fulfill these responsibilities. Any concerns regarding these should be brought to the attention of the group rather than discussing them individually with the group leader.

Members' Role and Responsibilities

1. By deciding to participate in this parent training program, each parent is making a commitment to attend the sessions and to receive help with childrearing concerns and difficulties. In addition to obtaining help for ourselves, we also are assuming responsibility for trying to give help to our fellow group members.

2. Each member has the ethical obligation to maintain confidentiality regarding what other members reveal about themselves and their personal concerns. In essence, we may discuss with others outside the counseling group setting only what personally involves ourselves and not that about other group members.

3. Because of the limited amount of time and the scope of the program, it is important that members arrive promptly and be present at all sessions. If persons are not able to attend a meeting, they are requested to notify the group leader in advance. All meetings will be started and concluded on time.

4. It is important that each member study the content materials and complete any homework suggested. This homework will be used for study and discussion purposes during the meetings.

5. In all group activities, respect and consideration for each other will be the by-word.

Group Discussion of Purpose and Format of the Program

(Discussion time: 5 minutes)

Understanding the purpose of the program and how the meetings will be conducted is essential for effective participation by members. Therefore, the following information needs to be thoroughly discussed and reviewed by the group.

Purpose and Format of the Program

1. The goal of *Developmental Childrearing* is to help parents acquire the knowledge, understandings, and skills important for positive childrearing and to use them for the benefit of their children and themselves.

2. Eight two-hour meetings will be held. Each meeting will consist of a 45-minute study phase, a 15-minute coffee break, and a group counseling session of one hour.

3. During the study phases, information about child development and childrearing practices will be explored. There will be time for discussions, questions, role playing, practice of some parenting techniques, and other activities involving member participation. Pertinent assignments to be carried out at home are included for most of the sessions. The emphasis in these study phases is upon understanding the information about children and childrearing and upon acquiring improved parenting skills. These periods are not for in-depth discussion of individual parenting concerns.

4. During the counseling group sessions, the emphasis will be upon individual childrearing concerns and mutual problem solving. The responsibility for what occurs during these counseling sessions—for receiving help and giving help—rests primarily upon the group members rather than upon the group leader.

Study Phase

(Discussion time: 15 minutes)

As children grow from infancy to adolescence, each age brings physical, social, emotional, and intellectual changes. In the process of growing up, all children follow the same predictable pattern of development. This development occurs in stages which are related directly to children's ages. Thus, children of the same ages tend to be in the same stages of development, engaging in similar behaviors, undergoing similar changes, and experiencing similar needs.

The term "needs" is used here to describe those conditions necessary to children for their maximum healthy development. Some needs arise during particular stages of development while others, such as the needs for safety and love, continue throughout life. Although each child is a unique individual, children of the same ages are alike in many of their needs and behaviors.

The concept of developmental stages is one which many parents have come to be aware of informally through their own observations of children. In comparing their childrearing experiences, parents whose children are close in age usually discover many likenesses in their children's behaviors and attitudes and in their own parenting concerns and difficulties. Parents' study of the stages of development in children can be helpful to them and beneficial to their children. Understanding these stages can enable parents to select and use parenting approaches to help children as they go through the stages and make life more enjoyable for the whole family.

Secondly, knowing what behaviors and possible difficulties to expect during a particular developmental stage can help parents to be prepared for what lies ahead. Understanding in advance the nature of these stages helps to alleviate parents' fears and frustrations as they try to cope with the rapidly changing needs and behaviors of growing children. This is especially advantageous when children go through a more difficult period of development and their behavior is frequently upsetting and trying.

Knowledge of the concept of behavioral stages of development in children is the result of extensive studies conducted by Dr. Arnold Gesell over a period of many years. He learned that children go through a series of behavioral stages which correspond to their ages. In other words, children grow in stages and the stages change with each age. All children experience these stages in the same order; no stage can be skipped or omitted. These stages are the result of the child's own maturation and the nature of the child's interactions with the personal environment. Here, the term "environment" refers to parents, siblings, family life style, and social, intellectual, and physical surroundings.

Furthermore, Gesell observed that the stages of behavioral development in children occur in a cycle. Initially, in each cycle, the child is in a stage of equilibrium or harmony when life goes quite smoothly. During this time, the child functions well, encountering few difficulties in daily living. In general, the child's attitudes toward self and others are positive and behavior is likely to be cooperative and pleasant, thus contributing to enjoyable family interactions.

This harmonious period is followed by a time of transition during which the child's behavior begins to break up or change. Difficulties in daily living begin to appear as the child develops less positive feelings about self and the world. These feelings become reflected in the child's attitudes and behaviors. Life for parent and child becomes less pleasant than during the previous stage.

The final stage of the cycle is a period of disequilibrium or disharmony. During these times, the child tends to encounter frequent difficulties, is unhappy about self and the world, and is hard to get along with. These are especially demanding and trying periods for parents and children.

It is important for parents to realize that these stages are natural and cannot be avoided. The child in a period of disharmony is not deliberately trying to make life difficult. Instead, the child is experiencing a normal stage of behavioral development. There is much that parents can do to help children proceed successfully through these stages, even the most exasperating ones. Related childrearing approaches will be presented during further meetings.

The study phases for this meeting and the following one contain descriptions of the behavioral stages of children ages five through ten according to Gessell. In this session, the focus is upon five and six year olds.

Five Year Olds

Five year olds are in a delightful stage of their development. During this period of equilibrium, they tend to be friendly, easy to get along with, and stable. Overall, this is a calm and contented time during which children feel secure about themselves and their world. This sense of security and well-being is apparent in their pleasing, cooperative behavior.

Children of this age are satisfied with staying at home in familiar surroundings rather than venturing out into unknown situations and settings. They are likely to undertake only those tasks which they are capable of accomplishing successfully, thus avoiding frustration and dissatisfaction.

Five year olds usually see mother as the favorite and most important person in their lives. As a result, they enjoy being with her, participating in activities with her, and doing things for her. Play is a major life activity for them, and they thrive on parental praise which is usually well-deserved because of their positive behavior during this period. Parents and children generally find the five year age a time of mutual enjoyment and satisfaction.

However, changes begin to occur as children approach the age of six. At about five and a half years of age, the calm and secure behavior of recent months begins to break up and a transition period is entered. Difficulties begin to develop, and children become less cooperative and less satisfied with themselves and their world. Parents wonder what has happened to their previously wonderful and enjoyable five year olds.

Six Year Olds

Six year olds are in a stage of development that is often difficult and frustrating to themselves and their parents. During this period, children are erratic; their feelings and behaviors quickly range from one extreme to the other. They change from love to hate, cooperation to defiance, and laughing to crying with unbelieveable speed and almost without warning. This is to be a time of explosive extremes for them.

Typically, children of this age are likely to be brash, aggressive, and self-centered. Along with this, they are demanding and inflexible, wanting things their own way and expecting others to meet their demands. They want to always be winners—to be the first, the best, to have the most, and to be loved the most.

This is a period when they seem to have boundless energy and are ready to undertake just about anything, even those tasks and activities which they are not yet developmentally ready to handle. They find it difficult to accept blame, criticism, or punishment for any reason, and when things go wrong, they see it as someone else's fault rather than their own. Daydreaming or fantasy is typical of children this age.

During this stage, their relationships with mother also change. She no longer continues to be the most important person; in fact, she become a frequent target of wrath when things go wrong. When life does not suit them, they tend to act as if it were her fault and take things out on her. During those infrequent times when life pleases them, however, they can be affectionate, cooperative, and warm.

It is helpful for parents going through this exasperating stage of their children's development to remember that this behavior is typical and normal for children this age. Their children are finding life difficult too. Mothers of six year olds are advised to sidestep confrontations with their children except on issues of critical importance. Also, whenever possible, other family members should become involved in helping with the care of the child. Fortunately, at approximately six and a half years of age, the rigid and uncooperative behavior which has been making life so stormy calms down somewhat.

Parent group members who have five and six year olds are urged to observe during the coming week their children's behavior in light of the study material presented in this session.

Homework Assignment:

Review for the next meeting the study phase information presented during the first meeting. Also, become familiar with the study phase information of the *Second Meeting*.

Break: (l5 minutes)

Counseling Phase: Session One

(Time: 60 minutes)

In this initial group counseling session, the group will begin to explore individual difficulties and problems in childrearing. Before beginning to do this, the group leader again will bring to the attention of the members the importance of maintaining confidentiality regarding what is discussed during these counseling sessions. Also, the members will be reminded of their responsibility to give as well as to receive help in dealing with concerns.

Following this, the leader will assist the members to discuss their personal childrearing concerns. Some parents may find this difficult to do at first for fear of appearing inadequate in some way. However, because the primary purpose for being in the group is to improve the quality of parenting, members need to participate actively in this process as soon as possible so that positve childrearing modifications may be begun.

It is important to remember that no childrearing concern is too trivial or too serious to be discussed in the counseling setting. More often than not, parents discover during such discussions many similarities in the nature of their concerns and are able to be understanding helpers for each other. Due to the newness of the situation, parents frequently feel a sense of uneasiness during this first counseling session. However, as the group begins to work together, such feelings usually disappear in a short time.

Through the use of counseling techniques, the group leader will assist the members to begin to feel more comfortable in the group and to communicate openly with each other. During this early stage of group counseling, members tend to look to the leader for immediate answers to their concerns. It is not the role of the leader to provide such answers. The primary responsibility lies with the counseling group members to find solutions for their difficulties, In this effort, it is important for members to bear in mind the information acquired during the study phases. Therefore, the group leader will avoid taking on the role of expert and problem solver. Instead, the leader will serve as a catalyst for the group, encouraging direct interactions between members and sharing the leadership role with participants whenever possible.

The Second Meeting

Before beginning the study phase of this meeting, parents should reintroduce themselves briefly. It is also advisable to take a few minutes to review members' roles and responsibilities as participants in the program. Emphasis should be placed upon the importance of the following member responsibilities in making this a worthwhile and beneficial experience:

1. promptness in arriving for the meetings,
2. regular attendance,
3. giving and receiving help for childrearing conerns,
4. confidentiality, and
5. completing homework assignments and the study phase material.

In order to avoid devoting undue time during study phases to the discussion of individual parenting concerns, members are reminded that these study phases are intended primarily for acquiring new information about child development, childrearing techniques, and skills development. The focus in the group counseling sessions during the latter part of each meeting is upon solving individual childrearing concerns and developing insights regarding parent-child interactions.

Study Phase

This study phase is for increasing parents' understanding of Gesell's stages and cycles of development in children. The first part of the lesson is devoted to the study of children ages seven through ten. Following this, an overview of children's needs and effective childrearing approaches for assisting them to progress successfully through the childhood years is presented.

Review: Because of the importance of the information about Gesell's theory presented during the study phase of the first meeting, a short review of the major concepts prior to discussion of new content is suggested. This should include the following:

1. All children follow the same predictable pattern of growth and development. This pattern consists of behavioral stages which occur in a cycle.

2. Knowing these stages can help parents to assist children to develop successfully. Also, the knowledge can help in dealing more effectively with future childrearing concerns and difficulties.

3. Because of individual differences in children, some variations in their behavior and in the timing of the onset of some stages may occur. However, in general, certain behaviors are typical of children of the same ages.

4. Children's behavior is affected by their own individual maturation and the nature of their interactions with parents and the environment.

5. The stages of behavior occur in a cycle which includes 1) a period of equilibrium or harmony, 2) a transition period, and 3) a period of disequilibrium or disharmony. During a period of equilibrium, children feel good about themselves and their world and life is generally pleasant. This is followed by a transition period in which children's behaviors, attitudes, and feelings start to change and difficulties begin to appear. Life is not quite so happy or smooth as before. Then a period of disequilibrium follows during which children tend to be unhappy with

themselves and their world. These difficult periods of disharmony present problems for both children and their parents.
6. The stages and cycles of behavior are natural. None can be skipped or avoided.
7. Five year olds are in a stage of equilibrium and harmony which starts to change at about age five and a half. Six year olds are in a period of disequilibrium which they and their parents find difficult and frustrating.

Discussion:

Parents of five and six year olds were asked during the first meeting to observe their children in terms of Gesell's descriptions of behavioral stages. A brief discussion of those parents' observations of their children's behavior is suggested before the group proceeds to the study of seven through ten year olds.

The Second Meeting

Seven Year Olds

The behavior of seven year olds generally is very different from the dynamic extremes of feelings and behavior of the six year old. Seven year olds are in a calmer, more withdrawn period and are a little easier to get along with. They tend to be observers rather than active participants and often prefer to be alone. They are likely to be tired, moody and morose; rarely are they the impatient, demanding, ready-for-action children they previously were. This is a time when they are concerned about themselves and how others treat them—a period of introspection.

During this stage, they are developing greater ability to concentrate and are more discriminating in their thinking and actions. They spend much time mulling things over and analyzing them. They now can sit quietly and listen for longer periods of time. They tend to be highly demanding of themselves, but they are not always able to complete tasks, even though they perservere for exhausting periods of time. Therefore, to avoid senseless frustration, children of this age need help in knowing when to stop. Seven year olds also like to be part of the group and do not want to be identified separately for either praise or blame.

The seven year old period has its high and low days. It is a time of many complaints by children who often feel that life is unfair to them. They are likely to complain that "others don't like me," "they hit me," they leave me out," or "they pick on me." These "others" include their parents and teachers as well as siblings and peers. Children of seven also frequently worry about things and are likely to be thoughtful, sensitive, and serious.

Parents can help by listening to their complaints with understanding and accepting them as real to their children. To seven year olds, their concerns are indeed valid and important. At the same time, however, wise parents will not take these problems too seriously, remembering that these difficulties are typical of seven year old children and an expected part of this developmental stage.

Eight Year Olds

The nature of this developmental age is in sharp contrast with the inward, withdrawn quality of the period preceding it. Eight year olds are characterized by enormous energy, activity, enthusiasm,, excitement, and curiosity. They are ready to meet life head on, to try new experiences, and to make new friends. Nothing seems too challenging or forbidding to them. Although they may become uspet temporarily when unsuccessful in particular efforts, they quickly rebound and forge ahead to new ventures.

Generally, their interests are of short duration, and they tend to become impatient to move on to new things. Eight year olds are likely to overestimate their own abilitiy in handling new tasks. This may result in severe self-criticism and tears when failure occurs. Therefore, they frequently need parental guidance to help them not to do too much and to deal with their own negative self-appraisals. Children of this age also need assistance from parents in understanding that all people experience failure sometimes and in planning activities appropriate to this developmental age.

Eight year olds care deeply about their relationships with others and want them to be good ones. They are concerned about what others think as well as do, rather than focusing mainly upon themselves as they did earlier. Their relationship with mother remains important to them and, although their peer group now plays an increasingly significant role in their lives, they still desire a close, caring relationship with her.

The Second Meeting

Nine Year Olds

At about the age of nine, this period of outwardness and exhuberance is replaced by a stage of greater inwardness and sureness. Nine year olds are in the process of developing increasing independence and self-sufficiency. They are more concerned now with their world outside the home and are more interested in the activities and opinions of friends than those of the family. They seek to be independent and demand to be considered mature and separate from the family. As part of this, they are likely to rebel against parental authority, especially in response to direct commands and bossing.

Their resistance generally is in the form of withdrawal or complaints as they do what has been requested of them. The emotional distance between nine year olds and their parents increases somewhat now as these children become more involved in the larger community and concerned with their membership in the peer group. This is a time of perfecting skills and high activity and interest in team sports and games.

Nine year olds are developing an increasing sense of truthfulness. They also tend to worry and take life very seriously. Things which formerly did not upset them now become sources of anxiety and concern. They are likely to complain often about physical ailments such as headaches and stomach aches. Although these are real to them and are not pretended, parents should become aware of the frequency with which these complaints accompany tasks disliked by their children. Nevertheless, these complaints are sincere and should not be ridiculed. They are children's natural ways of dealing with unpleasant situations and need to be handled with understanding, reason, and calm by parents. As children near the age of ten, the anxieties, complaints, and resistance of this stage become less frequent and intense.

Ten Year Olds

The anxieties and worries of the nine year stage disappear as children reach the age of ten. At this time, they enter a period of great equilibrium, one which is described as perhaps the most enjoyable stage in children's development. Ten year olds are very satisfied with themselves, their world, and especially their parents. They hold parents in high esteem and are cooperative and obedient in interactions with them. Gone is their resistance to parental authority shown so frequently during the previous stage. Now they enjoy pleasing their parents and do not question their guidance.

In general, ten year olds are dependable, cheerful, flexible, and affectionate. They treat others well and expect the same in return. Truthfulness continues to increase, and they no longer become upset by the many things which disturbed them earlier. They take life less seriously and are more practical and realistic.

This is a wonderful period in the lives of children and parents. Perhaps nature has provided it in preparation for the hectic and demanding pre-adolescent and adolescent stages which will follow.

Children's Needs and Effective Childrearing Approaches

In addition to the needs typical of children at each particular developmental age, all children experience some ongoing needs from birth to adulthood. Having these needs met satisfactorily is necessary for healthy child development. The following section describes these needs and suggests effective childrearing approaches for each.

1. **Children need love.**

    Childrearing Approach: Show love and affection to your children. A warm hug, a kiss, a touch, or the words "I love you" are necessary for the healthy development of children at all ages. They are as important to the wellbeing of older children as to younger ones and to boys as well as to girls.

2. Children need understanding and acceptance as unique, growing persons.

Childrearing Approach: Take the time to communicate with your children. Listen to their ideas and feelings and let them know that you understand how they feel. Allow them the right to their own feelings. Too often when children relate to adults feelings such as fear or anger, we tend to ridicule them or to reject their feelings. A parent response such as, "Only babies are afraid of thunder" or, "Of course, you're not really mad at Mommy" thwart open communication between parents and children and contribute to children's feelings of being misunderstood and unaccepted.

Also, it is essential for parents to keep in mind the fact that each child is unique. Even children within the same family are different from each other. This uniqueness should be accepted and encouraged. Denying children their individuality causes them to experience feelings of inadequacy and excessive competition and results in undesirable behavior such as aggressiveness, withdrawal, oversubmissiveness, and psychosomatic symptoms. Therefore, parents should avoid such tactics as comparing children to siblings or peers. A parent comment to a child such as, "Your brother never did such naughty things when he was your age" is destructive.

3. Children need to develop competency.

Childrearing Approach: As they grow, children are naturally inclined to want to learn and to master new tasks. The accomplishment of these leads to feelings of competency and competent behavior. Therefore, it is critical that parents provide children with opportunities for informal and formal learning appropriate to their level of development and their interests.

When children ask questions or show curiosity about a particular subject, parents can help them to learn by responding to the extent of the children's understanding. As they express the desire to undertake new tasks or activities, parental encouragement for those efforts suitable to their developmental stage assists children to become increasingly competent and independent. Appropriate activities such as games, sports, trips, reading, scouting, interest clubs, films, and experiences in the performing and visual arts should be made available.

Children discouraged by parents from developing new competencies for reasons of overprotection or overrestrictiveness become unsure of themselves. They also become fearful and overdependent upon parents and others. They feel incompetent and behave accordingly. To avoid this, parents should approach children's desires to try new things from a practical and rational viewpoint. Consideration should be given to the child's readiness for the task and the possible dangers involved.

For example, the five year old living in a quiet, residential neighborhood who wants to play with the children across the street can be taught how to cross the street safely. When mastery of this task has been shown consistently over a period of time, the child can be allowed to do so alone with the understanding that mother be informed when one is going to do this so that she knows where the child is. This type of learning experience helps the child to feel and to become competent.

On the other hand, for the five year old who lives on a very busy thoroughfare, this might be inadvisable. If so, a clear and logical explanation by the parent regarding the conditions involved should be given and an agreeable substitute method arrived at jointly by parent and child.

4. Children need to feel secure.

Childrearing Approach: Parents can help children to feel secure by setting and maintaining rules for living and limits for behavior which are reasonable and appropriate to the individual child's developmental stage. As children mature, these must be reviewed and modified periodically to meet their increasing need for independence and responsibility. Care should be taken during each stage to avoid parental overpermissiveness or overrestrictiveness, both of which are equally damaging to children.

When fair and suitable rules and limits have been established by parents and are understood by children, it is of critical importance that children be assisted to adhere to them consistently. A lack of parental consistency in maintaining rules for living causes children to believe that life is unpredictable and confusing and that parents cannot be depended upon. These conclusions result in feelings of fearfulness and anxiety on the part of children and in their constant testing of limits to discover what they may expect of parents and others.

Developmental Childrearing

5. Children need to be responsible, contributing members of the family.

Childrearing Approach: In order for children to develop feelings of competency, belonging, and significance, it is necessary that they contribute in positive ways to the ongoingness of family life. Children should be given responsibilities and duties within the family compatible with their ages and abilities which they may carry out successfully. As part of this, parent expectations that these responsibilities will be performed regularly should be conveyed clearly to children. In the event that children neglect to do so, parents must firmly and calmly see to it that these obligations are met.

Giving children appropriate responsibility for contributing constructively to family living should be begun when they are young. Even young children are able to accomplish certain tasks such as putting away toys, helping to set the table, and unpacking groceries. The patterns of responsible behavior begun during these early years tend to be maintained during later life stages.

6. **Children need to experience success in most undertakings, with an occassional failure from which to learn about the reality of life.**

   Childrearing Approach: In general, children need to be successful in what they do in order to develop feelings of competency. This applies to experiences at home, in school, and in the community. However, an occasional failure can be helpful rather than damaging to children. Through such experiences, parents can help children to learn that it is okay not to be perfect and that all people, even parents, fail at times. When failure occurs, parents should convey understanding of the child's feelings and provide encouragement for future efforts in that area when the child appears to be ready.

7. **Children need parental discipline which allows parents and children to maintain their dignity and integrity.**

   Childrearing Approach: The utimate purpose of parental discipline is to help children become responsible, independent, and effective adults. In view of this goal, the best techniques are those which help children to develop positive attitudes and behaviors in regard to themselves and others.

   Disciplining children on an emotional level, such as humiliating, shaming, ridiculing, threatening, yelling, and hitting, should be avoided. Although these may sometimes seem to be the easiest ways for parents and may achieve conformity, they are extremely destructive for children.

   Parents are urged to employ methods of discipline which are suitable to children's ages and understanding and which allow all parties to maintain self-respect. An effective approach for parents to use includes the following: 1) a calm explanation of the reasons the particular behavior of the child is unacceptable; 2) suggestions by parent and child regarding alternative behaviors; and 3) mutual agreement upon an alternative behavior. If the offending behavior persists, the parent should calmly use reasonable measures such as removing the child from the situation. In selecting such measures, consideration should be given to the child's level of development and understanding.

   For example, depriving a five year old of outdoor play for two weeks for continuing not to come home when called is inappropriate for a child this age. Young children respond better to immediate and short-term measures because of their short attention span. Therefore, a shorter approach and one which is directly related to the offending act would be more appropriate and effective.

Homework Assignment:

Review thoroughly the information presented during the first two study phases. Select one of the childrearing approaches recommended in this session and use it with your child during this coming week. Please remember that your continued and consistent use over time of the approach you choose is necessary in order for it to be effective. Therefore, please do not expect immediate changes to occur.

Be prepared to report at our next meeting about the following:

1. Which childrearing method did you select?
2. Why did you chose that particular one?
3. Describe the steps you took in carrying out that method with your child.
4. Describe your child's responses to your efforts.
5. How did you feel while doing these things?
6. What will you do to continue using this method?
7. Which of the other childrearing methods do you feel ready to try?

It is also suggested that you take a look at the study phase material of the *Third Meeting* prior to the next session.

Break: (15 minutes)

Counseling Phase: Session Two

Group members usually have begun to feel more comfortable with each other by the time the second counseling session begins. However, because the group is still in the initial stage of its development, a true sense of group cohesion has not yet been achieved. Therefore, members continue to try to clarify, each in their own way, what behaviors are actually acceptable in this counseling setting. They are still trying to discover what the other members are like, to what extent it is advisable to be open and trusting, and what roles the various members will play in the group. Also, members still tend to turn to the group leader for solutions to problems and are more likely to direct their comments to that person than to each other. By the end of this second session, most groups are well on the way to successfully resolving these issues.

The process of developing a growth-producing group characterized by trust and openness can be enhanced by members' efforts to share responsibility with the professional leader for what happens in the group. This requires not only examining one's own childrearing concerns but also helping other members to express and explore theirs. The group leader will model some counseling techniques to help members interact with each other and develop greater awareness of feelings and attitudes toward children and themselves as parents. This self-awareness is essential in order for parents to improve their childrearing skills and attitudes.

Two counseling techniques most likely to assist members in the development of self-awareness are 1) empathic listening, i.e. listening for members' feelings as they talk, and 2) reflecting feelings; i.e., showing understanding of these feelings. The group leader will use these frequently throughout the counseling sessions. Through observation of the leader's use of these techniques, group members generally acquire skill and fluency in their use and become able to employ them in interactions with each other. Members will find that the use of these techniques outside the group is helpful for improving the quality of communication and relationships with both children and adults.

Empathic listening requires that the listener understands the verbal content of the speaker's message, and, along with this, understands how the speaker feels about the subject. This necessitates that the listener concentrate on what is being said and also how it is being said. Through the use of empathy— putting yourself in the other person's shoes in order to understand feelings—the listener is able to comprehend the total message being conveyed by the person speaking.

For example, the father of an eight year old child makes the following statement: "It seems as if every time we tell Billy to do something, he does just the opposite. We have tried everything—from coaxing to spankings—but nothing seems to work."

The verbal message here is that these parents have tried unsuccessfully in a variety of ways to gain cooperation from their son. The feelings of that father seem to be frustration and discouragement.

If the initial statement is not clear to the listener(s), further information may be sought by asking questions of the sender, in this case, the father. After the message has been clarified adequately, the technique called reflecting feelings can be used to show understanding of the total message; i.e., the verbal content of the message and the underlying feelings of the sender. The following is an example of a response to that father by another group member in which reflecting feelings is used. "You feel discouraged about changing Billy's behavior because nothing you have tried seems to have made a difference."

Understanding of both the feeling (discouraged) and the verbal message (have tried unsuccessfully to resolve the difficulty) have been transmitted back to the father. This type of responding can help others to develop self-understanding and self-awareness, the necessary first steps for beginning to deal effectively with childrearing concerns.

As group members, parents should take the opportunity during counseling sessions to observe carefully these techniques as they are modeled by the group leader. Also, members should attempt to use them regularly in communicating with other members. Early efforts at using them are likely to seem stiff and unnatural at first. However, continued practice will enable you to feel comfortable with them so that eventually they will become an integral part of your communication skills. Time will be devoted during a future meeting to parents' utilization of these approaches in interacting with children.

Sometimes, during this second counseling session, some group members may begin to consider possible solutions for their problems. When this occurs, every effort should be made to develop solutions which are based upon information from the study phases and are feasible for the parent to carry out. However, in most groups, actual problem solving usually takes place during later sessions after the members have had adequate time for discussing concerns and engaging in self-exploration.

The Third Meeting

Study Phase

This study phase is devoted primarily to becoming familiar with Erik Erikson's psychosocial stages of development in children from birth to age twelve. The group will learn also about childrearing approaches for fostering children's emotional and social development in view of these stages. Prior to studying Erikson's theory, time is allocated for members to report their experiences in carrying out the homework assignment of the previous session.

Discussion of Homework Assignment

In discussing the homework assignment of using one of the suggested childrearing methods, attention should be given to the following as the members report their experiences:

1. The parenting approach selected and the reason for choosing that particular one.
2. Strategies used by the parent in carrying out the approach.
3. Reactions of children to these strategies.
4. Parents' feelings regarding their use of the approaches.
5. Future plans for continuing these efforts.
6. Selection of an additional approach to be tried.

During this discussion, the group should assist members to identify successes, possible reasons for difficulties encountered, and ways for resolving these difficulties. Emphasis should be given to the fact that 1) the consistent use of these methods over a considerable period of time is required in order to achieve lasting benefits and 2) whenever anyone attempts to change attitudes and behaviors, time, effort, and patience are necessary. Parents are encouraged to continue the approaches already begun and to begin an additional method appropriate to their individual childrearing concerns (See Item 6 above).

Erikson's Psychosocial Stages of Development

Erik Erikson observed that the emotional and social development of human beings occurs in stages which begin at birth and continue throughout life. These psychosocial stages follow a specific sequence, with each being more complex than the previous one. In order to develop to the greatest extent, the individual must progress satisfactorily through each succeeding stage.

During each psychosocial stage of development, there is a particular crisis or task which must be accomplished successfully. (For purposes of this discussion, "crisis" will be used hereafter to refer to this concept of social-emotional tasks.) If a person masters adequately the crisis of each earlier stage, this contributes to the likelihood of success in later stages, However, it does not definitely insure later success.

Failure to resolve successfully the crisis of an earlier stage causes individuals to experience difficulties in subsequent stages. This is because they continue to try to accomplish the tasks which should have been mastered previously. Thus, they are deterred from using their full energies to deal with the crisis of their present stage. In some cases, successful resolution of these psychosocial crises is never achieved, and the person experiences a variety of ongoing social-emotional difficulties throughout life.

Parents can do a great deal to help their children achieve healthy emotional and social development in each of the stages. In fact, parents are a major influence in this process during the formative years of childhood. The following sections of this study phase describe the psychosocial stages of development in children from birth to age twelve and how parents can promote children's successful development in each stage.

Stage One-Psychosocial Crisis: Developing a Sense of Trust Versus a Sense of Mistrust, Birth to One Year of Age

During the first year of life, the psychosocial crisis to be resolved is the development of an attitude of trust rather than one of mistrust. The sense of trust or mistrust formed during this period affects children's present and future feelings, attitudes, and behaviors. Developing a sense of trust of self, parents, and the world around them during this year is the basic foundation for healthy social-emotional development and functioning in future years.

The parents, or surrogate parents, play a crucial role during this psychosocial stage as well as during the following stages of childhood and adolescence. The behaviors and attitudes of parents in interacting with children are the key factors in how successfully infants resolve the psychosocial crisis of this stage. In order for them to develop a basic attitude of trust toward themselves and others, they need consistency in the love, attitudes, physical care, comforting, modes of interacting, daily routine of living, and other experiences provided by parents. Consistency in these areas of living enables children to feel loved, accepted, and secure and to believe that their world is safe and predictable. These feelings and beliefs are essential for the development of a basic attitude of trust.

In essence, the development of trust is the result of feeling loved and well cared for along with knowing what to expect from parents and the environment. A sense of mistrust is developed when the baby is treated inconsistently, such as being cuddled and comforted by mother when crying because of discomfort and then being ignored by her the next time this situation occurs. Babies whose parents are inconsistent in their behaviors and attitudes or who are deprived of love, abused, or neglected become distrustful of themselves and others, suspicious, and anxious. They develop a basic attitude of mistrust which causes them to experience problems in the present and contributes to developmental difficulties in the future.

Stage Two-Psychosocial Crisis: Developing a Sense of Autonomy Versus a Sense of Shame and Doubt: Ages One to Two

Between the ages of one and two, the psychosocial crisis of children is to develop a sense of autonomy rather than one of shame and doubt. This sense of autonomy requires that the child becomes more self-directive, independent, and assertive rather than remaining the helpless infant. It is during this period of development that children begin to walk and move around quite easily, acquire increased language skills, and understand much of what they hear. At the same time, they develop better use of their hands and have an insatiable curiosity to learn about the world around them.

Suddenly parents find themselves confronted with decisions about how to deal with these active, assertive children who seem to want to get into everything and have strong opinions about what they will and will not do. The general childrearing approaches adopted at this time have great impact upon children's developing a sense of autonomy.

Constructive childrearing in this stage requires parents' use of encouragement and willingness to allow reasonable freedom for children to express themselves and to explore their environment. They need to be permitted to develop and indicate their own preferences, likes, and dislikes and to begin to feel some control over themselves and what they do. It is important also that they be allowed to move about the home, to touch things, and to find out how they work.

These suggestions do not imply allowing children complete freedom to do whatever they desire. Overpermissiveness by parents is as damaging to children's development as are overprotection and rigid authoritarianism. Instead, it is essential that parents allow children freedom within limits, providing firm and consistent guidance to protect them from experiences and environmental hazards for which they are not yet ready. It is also advisable for parents to make their homes as child-safe as possible during this period.

If children are allowed to come to view themselves as persons in their own right, although still dependent upon their parents, the sense of autonomy develops satisfactorily. Along with this, their competency and feelings of trust increase. Conversely, if children feel disapproval in their efforts to develop autonomy, they will feel unsure of themselves, inadequate, and powerless. These negative and destructive feelings continue into future life stages and are reflected in children's constantly seeking help and looking to others to do things for them.

Stage Three-Psychological Crisis: Developing a Sense of Initiative Versus a Sense of Guilt: Ages Three to Five

The psychosocial task of these pre-schoolers is to develop a sense of initiative rather than one of guilt. The sense of initiative includes mastery of new tasks, responsibility, self-confidence, resourcefulness, and resilience. During this period of development, children typically seek new experiences and want to undertake new tasks. They are highly motivated to learn and tend to imitate adults in their behaviors and play activities. At this life stage, children become sexually curious, develop a sense of conscience, and begin to discriminate between right and wrong. They also have fantasies of personal power as well as tendencies to feel guilty about wrong-doing or failure.

Parents can do much to enhance the development of three to five year olds. Their sense of initiative is encouraged by allowing them to attempt challenging new tasks within their realm of possible accomplishment. If failure occurs, they should be allowed to experience it without being made to feel guilty and opportunities provided to try again when they indicate interest in doing so. Learning to bounce back from failure still feeling good about themselves is vital to them. It is imperative that parents avoid playing upon children's sense of guilt in order to gain conformity to expected behavior. Parents' use of methods which employ guilt to make children do what they want or to curtail undesired behavior severely restricts healthy development.

Children of this age benefit from being given real and reasonable responsibilities which they can manage successfully. Examples of such responsibilities are caring for belongings and pets, setting the table, and helping to clean the yard—all of which make them feel like worthwhile, contributing members of the family.

It is important that they do assigned tasks regularly and be allowed enough time to complete them, even though it may seem more expedient to take over for them when they dawdle. Attitudes toward self as a competent and responsible worker and behavioral patterns of completing tasks have their origins during these years.

If the sense of initiative does not develop adequately during this time, children are likely to feel guilty about their goals, lack spontaneity, and become suspicious and evasive. The keys to good parenting during this and later developmental stages are love, consistency, encouragement, respect, and reasonable demands and limits.

Stage Four-Psychological Crisis: Developing a Sense of Industry Versus a Sense of Inferiority: Ages Six through Eleven

The psychosocial crisis of children ages six through eleven is to acquire the skills, competencies, and understandings necessary for them to function effectively in their world. Although the role of parents and family continues to be important to their development, teachers and peers also exert great influence upon them during this stage. Because of this importance of school and peers, their performance in academic and social areas and in activities valued by peers has significant impact upon the development of a sense of industry.

The sense of industry may best be conceptualized as feelings of competency and self-worth; a sense of inferiority involves feelings of incompetency, ineffectiveness, and unimportance. To adequately develop a sense of industry, children of elementary school age must acquire the concepts, information, and skills necessary for academic achievement. They also must gain the skills and competencies to participate well in social relationships and in activities of their peers, such as sports, music, games, and so forth.

There are additional important tasks which children must accomplish at this time. They must learn to put off immediate gratification in order to reach larger goals. An example of this is being willing and able to save one's allowance for a period of time to purchase a particular item later rather than spending it as it is received. As they mature during these years, children also must become less egocentric, learning to give of themselves to others and to be concerned about others. Along with these tasks, they must learn to develop personal values and to make value judgments.

Adults can do much to help elementary school children successfully resolve the psychosocial crisis of developing a sense of industry as opposed to a sense of inferiority. Parents and teachers need to provide opportunities for them to engage in meaningful and worthwhile tasks and to develop skills and abilities in academic, social, recreational, and cultural areas of living.

They need to experience productivity, task completion, and general success in what they do. Of course, it is neither possible nor advisable for adults to protect children from occasional setbacks or minor failures. What is important is that children be provided work and experiences in which they are successful most of the time. When setbacks or disappointments do occur from time to time, adults should help them to understand that all people experience these sometimes. They also should provide opportunities for developing the necessary skills and encouragement for future efforts.

Parents and teachers can help children to develop a sense of industry by giving them increasing responsibility and by allowing and encouraging them to make decisions and solve problems. As they progress through these years, children should be involved expandingly in making decisions and solving difficulties related to school; recreational and social activities and interests; time allocations for play, homework, and household chores; choices of clothing; plans for family trips and activities; spending money; and friends and interpersonal relationships.

Adults important in their lives serve as role models for children. The behaviors, attitudes, values, and beliefs of parents and teachers serve as standards for children during these formative years. They are influenced through their observations of what parents and teachers say and do and even by what is left unspoken or undone by them. As a result of these observations, children arrive at their own conclusions regarding many aspects of life. Inconsistencies between what we tell our children is right and what we ourselves do cause confusion for them and thus should be avoided.

For example, parents who forbid their children to hit younger siblings, saying that it is wrong to hit someone smaller than oneself, but who themselves use hitting as punishment are presenting a conflicting picture for their youngsters. Parents and teachers must make every effort to exemplify the kinds of behaviors, attitudes, values, and beliefs they hope children will learn.

Children continue to need a consistent, secure, and loving home environment as well as understanding and firm guidance from parents throughout these years. If the critical psychosocial crisis of industry versus inferiority is not accomplished sufficiently, children will not concentrate well on tasks, will be careless and disorganized in their work, and will tend to avoid competitive situations. All of these can have undesirable outcomes for them as children as well as later during adulthood.

Homework Assignment:

Review the study information presented during this meeting. Concentrate especially upon the description of the stage your child is in; this should be determined according to the child's age. Based upon your perceptions of your child, list what steps you are willing to take to enhance success during this stage. Then prioritize these by assigning the numeral one to the most important step, two to the second most important step, and so forth. Bring this listing to use in the next session. Also scan the content of the fourth study phase in preparation for the next meeting.

Break: (15 minutes)

Counseling Phase: Session Three

During this session, the group members continue to discuss their personal childrearing concerns and to consider approaches for dealing with them. Members feel quite comfortable and safe with each other and with the leader at this third session, and most are actively involved in the group effort. They now listen and respond to each other more constructively, applying new insights about child development and childrearing methods acquired from the study materials to the problems brought to the group. In doing so, members benefit by developing greater self-awareness and new understandings about themselves and their children. Although it may seem as if the group is at a plateau and is showing little movement, in actuality, the group is progressing into the working stage during which decisions will be made and carried out.

Occasionally, during this third counseling session, some members begin to feel impatient that they have not yet made greater gains in resolving their difficulties and wonder about continuing in the group. They seem to feel the need for immediate action regarding their concerns rather than spending this time upon exploring feelings, attitudes, and difficulties. Should this impatience occur, it is helpful for the group to discuss it so that support, understanding, and encouragement may be provided for these members' continuing participation.

The Fourth Meeting

Study Phase

In this meeting, the study of personality development in children according to Alfred Adler will begin. Emphasis will be upon children's goals and behavior, why they act as they do, the role of family and home life, and the effect of birth order positions upon children. The study of the Adlerian theory will continue over the next several study phases. For parents interested in more extensive information about the Adlerian approach to childrearing than is provided in this program, *Children: the Challenge* by R. Dreikurs and V. Stoltz (1964) is suggested.

Prior to beginning the actual study phase, fifteen minutes are allocated for group discussion of the homework assignment.

Discussion of Homework Assignment

Members should have brought with them their prioritized lists of what they might do to enhance their children's success in resolving the psychosocial crisis of their stages of development. Attention should be given by the group to the two items ranked first on each person's list.

The group should assist members to describe in specific behavioral terms what they intend to do to implement the two items each has identified as most important on their lists. For example, to help the nine year old child to develop a sense of industry versus a sense of inferiority, what new responsibilities is the parent going to give to the child? How does the parent plan to do this? How will the parent provide recognition of the child's successful accomplishment of these? What will the parent do if the child does not carry out the new responsibilities? What will the parent do if the child is not yet able to accomplish a specific task assigned? At the close of the discussion, members should be ready to carry out at home the two approaches they have explored with the group.

Personality Development: The Adlerian Theory

It is likely that many parents question from time to time what causes children to be as they are and to behave as they do. Those who have more than one child are keenly aware of the differences in the children's personalities and behaviors even though they are being reared in the same environment. Many theories have been formulated to explain personality development and human behavior. The theory of Alfred Adler, a pioneer in the field of child guidance, is especially useful for helping parents to understand how personality develops in children, the goals for their behavior, and the role parents play in this process.

According to Adler's theory, a number of factors are influential upon the development of children's personality and behavior. These include the following: 1) the life goals which motivate human behavior; 2) the personal motives developed by each child; 3) how the child interprets personal experiences; 4) types of life styles; 5) the family atmosphere; 6) the family constellation and the child's birth order position; and 7) the kind of parenting and family which the child experiences.

During this and the next two meetings, Adler's theory of personality development and strategies to foster healthy personality development and behavior in children will be presented. In the study material for this meeting, attention is focused upon the first six of the factors noted above which impact upon personality development in children.

The Ultimate Goals of Behavior

All human behavior is goal oriented; that is, it has purpose. When children behave as they do, their behavior is influenced by two types of goals—those which are common to all children and those which are unique to each child. The goals shared by all children are known as the ultimate goals of behavior.

Children are constantly trying to achieve these ultimate life goals although they are not consciously aware of them. It is important that parents understand the nature of these primary goals so that they may provide the kind of childrearing and family life which assists children to move toward successful achievement of these goals.

There are three ultimate life goals universal to children. The first of these is to attain a sense of significance; this refers to feelings of being important and unique in one's particular world. Secondly, they seek to achieve a sense of belonging— feelings of have close, cooperative relationships with others and being an essential member of the family group. Their third goal is to be able to cope successfully with the demands and problems of living which they encounter. This entails developing the skills and competencies necessary for effective functioning in everyday living. Even when they are very young, children unconsciously try to reach these goals.

The extent to which these goals of significance, belonging, and competency are attained during childhood depends greatly upon children's experiences within the family, particularly during the first five years of life. The nature and quality of their interactions and relationships with parents and other family members and their ability to successfully meet demands and expectations in this setting are of critical importance. Although experiences during the first five years of life are especially significant to children's development, these two factors continue to influence them throughout the childhood years.

If children are successful for the most part in interpersonal relationships and in accomplishing the many tasks expected of them by parents and significant others, a sense of significance, belongingness, and competency results. Conversely, if they experience ongoing difficulties in relationships, especially within the family, and frequently fail to master certain tasks or to fulfill expectations, children come to feel unimportant, incompetent, discouraged, and left out. Such children tend to withdraw from those areas of living in which they have been unsuccessful and limit themselves only to areas where they feel a sense of belongingness.

Fictional Finalisms

In addition to these ultimate goals of behavior which motivate all children, each individual child also unconsciously forms specific, personal goals. These are known as fictional finalisms. They are long range goals and may be best thought of as motives for behavior. Examples of fictional finalisms are: the desire to be more intelligent, more beautiful, more respected, more athletic, and so forth.

The fictional finalisms adopted by children are derived from the convictions and beliefs they form about themselves and their world during their early years. In their efforts to attain a sense of significance, belonging, and competence, they observe and interpret their experiences. As a result of this processing, they reach unconscious conclusions regarding how best to fit into their world.

Fictional finalisms are based upon these conclusions and become powerful motives for children's behavior. For example, if a child unconsciously determines from personal observations and experiences that the way to be important and to achieve belongingness in the family is to be the smartest child, the child's behavior will be aimed at achieving this goal.

If children's convictions and beliefs are true and based upon reality, they are able to function effectively. However, if they operate under misunderstandings and mistaken beliefs about themselves, others, and the methods for finding a place in life, they experience difficulties in related areas of living and tend to become unhappy and discouraged.

For children who adopt unrealistic or negative fictional finalisms, life can become frustrating and destructive. Those who conclude that the only way to belong and be important and effective is by being the naughtiest or the most troublesome child in the family establish negative behavior patterns. These can eventually result in their becoming completely discouraged and giving up on themselves. When children form beliefs about themselves and their world, whether true or mistaken, they act as if they are true and their only possible choice.

Biased Apperception or Faulty Logic

In addition to the kinds of relationships and experiences children have during their early formative years, another factor is involved in determining the kinds of beliefs and convictions children develop about themselves and life. This is known as biased apperception or faulty logic. It refers to the phenomenon that each child sees life from a personally unique point of view.

Children interpret their experiences and observations in terms of their own individual perceptions and respond to what suits their own purposes. They decide for themselves, according to their own individual interpretations and goals, the meaning and importance of the many elements in their lives. This personal perceiving greatly influences the conclusions children form about themselves, others, and their place in the world.

Lifestyles

In the Adlerian theory of personality development, the term "lifestyle" is used to describe personality. Adler viewed lifestyle as the distinctive way in which an individual moves through life; it encompasses feelings, thought processes, attitudes, and behaviors.

The development of one's lifestyle begins at birth and is influenced by both heredity and environment. In addition, it is affected by the individual's personal perceptions and conclusions about the many aspects of living. The individual is considered to be an active agent in determining one's own unique lifestyle rather than being passively molded by genetic and environmental factors alone.

Because of this interaction of heredity, environment, and personal perceptions, each person develops a lifestyle or personality distinctively different from all others. Adler identified two general types of lifestyles: 1) the constructive lifestyle and 2) the destructive lifestyle. Each has its own goals, characteristics, and typical behaviors.

Constructive lifestyles are characterized by cooperation, feelings of competency and belonging, and interest in and extensive interaction with others. Children who develop constructive lifestyles are generally cooperative, feel capable of solving most of the problems of living which they encounter, and also feel that they occupy a special place in their world. They are social beings who are interested in and enjoy relating to others. The general goal of the constructive lifestyle is the attainment of attention and service.

Within the broad category of constructive lifestyle or personality, there are two specific types. The first of these is the active constructive lifestyle. Children who develop this type of personality are ambitious and oriented to success. They obtain attention and service for what they accomplish. The second type of constructive lifestyle is the passive constructive lifestyle. Children with this kind of personality are charming and receive attention for what they are rather than what they do.

On the other hand, destructive lifestyles are typified by competition, insecurity, jealousy, and inadequate feelings of competency and belonging. There are two particular types of destructive lifestyles—active and passive. Children who acquire active destructive lifestyles are discouraged, rebellious, and revengeful; they continuously challenge the authority of parents and others. If a passive destructive is formed, children feel discouraged, sometimes to the extent of hopelessness. They limit their interactions with others and withdraw from those areas of living in which they feel inadequate.

There are four goals or fictional finalisms for the destructive lifestyles. They are:

1. Attaining attention or service
2. Cancelling out the power of others

3. Obtaining revenge

4. Seeking to be left alone; giving up and withdrawing

As you may have noted, the first of these goals, the attainment of attention or service, is also the goal of constructive lifestyles. However, the remaining three goals are applicable only to destructive lifestyles. These goals and the process through which they become adopted by children will be more thoroughly described in the study material of the fifth meeting.

The Family Atmosphere

The family atmosphere during the early years of life contributes significantly to the development of children's lifestyles. The family atmosphere is the characteristic pattern of living established by parents. It serves for children as the standard for social living. In essence, children are exposed to society through parents and the family atmosphere they maintain which reflects the religious, racial, economic, social, and political values they hold. Parents convey to children their personal philosophy and concepts about life through their own behavior in family relationships. The bases for sex roles, values, attitudes, patterns of behavior, and modes of interactions are communicated to the children through the family atmosphere.

The methods adopted by children in their striving toward belonging, significance, and competency are determined partly by the family atmosphere. If the atmosphere is characterized by cooperation, mutual trust, and respect, children are encouraged to establish a constructive life style. An atmosphere of distrust, competition, and disrespect tends to foster the adoption of a destructive lifestyle. Whether children will be active or passive in efforts to achieve their goals depends upon the extent to which the family atmosphere stresses personal initiative. Where personal initiative is emphasized in the family, children are likely to be active in these efforts. Values, patterns of relationships, and modes of behavior shared by children in the same family are outcomes of the influence of the same family atmosphere.

The Family Constellation

The nature of the family constellation also has a profound effect upon the personality development of children. Family constellation refers to the social and emotional makeup of the family; it consists of such factors as the personal characteristics of each member, the emotional distances of the members from each other, family size, ages and sexes of the children, and the order of birth of each child. Differences in lifestyle among children in the same family may be attributed in part to the fact that each child occupies a unique position in the family and interprets life from that special vantage point.

The singularity of each child's position in the family is of key importance in the process of personality development. Each child occupies a distinctly different position in the family due to 1) the child's own personal influence upon the other members and 2) varying conditions within the family as each child is born.

As discussed previously in the section on lifestyles, children are not merely the products of their heredity and environment. Although these factors play an important role in personality development, children themselves are active agents in the process. In their striving toward the ultimate goals of significance, belonging, and competency, they influence others to treat them as they expect to be treated.

Acting upon their personal conclusions about themselves and others, they behave in ways which contribute to determining the nature of their place in the family. In addition to the personal influence of the child, changing conditions within the family as children are born also cause each child's position in the family to be different. With the birth of each child, the parents change; they become older, more experienced, more or less secure, more or less discouraged, and so forth. In some instances, family income changes or an older relative moves into the home. A new baby may be the only one of that sex among the siblings. Because of such factors as these, each child occupies a different position in the family and actually grows up in a different situation.

Birth Order

Children's interpretations of and responses to their birth order positions in the family have an influence upon the development of their personalities. According to the Adlerian theory, the child's birth position in the configuration of the family tends to produce certain characteristics. This means that similarities of personality are shown by children holding the same birth order position in their respective families. These are due to the fact that the child's birth position provides special opportunities which are used in the relationships established with other family members. Within the family, children measure their status and competency by comparing themselves to their siblings.

The five ordinal positions of birth order are: 1) oldest, 2) second, 3) middle, 4) youngest, and 5) the only. One child may have two positions—the second and the youngest. A child may hold one of these positions for a period of years and then have a new one. A younger child who is brighter and more favored than an older child symbolically may occupy a position different from the actual birth order position and may assume the position of the oldest.

Oldest children are viewed as being preoccupied with maintaining a position of being first or best. Often they have difficulty when the second child arrives and they are no longer the center of their parents' attention. As a result, they may experience feelings of neglect, insecurity, and being unloved. If this occurs and they fail to obtain attention through positive behavior, they are likely to try less desirable tactics.

Second children are always trying to catch up with and pass the oldest child. If they are not able to succeed, they may give up and become lazy or discouraged. Generally, second children will develop skills in areas where the oldest children are not strong. Because of this, it is usual for first and second siblings to have opposite characteristics. The greatest competition between siblings generally exists between the first two children in the family. In fact, these two children tend to influence each other more than their parents do. Sometimes parents, not understanding this sibling competition, tend to reinforce it and their children's false assumptions about success and failure rather than stressing cooperation and respect for individuality.

Middle children do not have the rights of the oldest nor the privileges of the youngest. Because of this, they frequently feel neglected and discriminated against in their efforts to achieve a sense of belonging, significance, and competency. If they become strongly discouraged, they are likely to resort to adopting mistaken goals of behavior and act in ways which are destructive to themselves.

Youngest children usually assume one of two roles. Some play the role of the pampered, overindulged baby who is the family boss, obtaining service and attention by cuteness and helplessness. On the other hand, others take the direction of outdoing their siblings in an attempt to compensate for their own self-perceived weaknesses. If parents prevent their youngest children from taking on responsibility and making decisions, they tend to feel inferior and incompetent and conclude that others are always more capable, stronger, and wiser than they are.

Those who are the only child have a special situation, living solely with others who are larger and more capable than they. For some, this results in their attempting to develop skills and abilities in areas that will gain adult approval. Sometimes, however, only children seek attention and service by being shy, timid, or helpless.

Special family situations affect this pattern of birth order positions. If there is a span of several years between births, the oldest child in the second group of siblings may develop characteristics of an oldest child in the family. If the first and second born children are of different sexes, each may assume traits of the oldest child. In larger families, there often are several small groupings of children which have the characteristics of a small family.

The striving for security and belonging of each sibling may lead to competition or alliances between them. When a child sees a sibling as a threat to one's own status, competition develops. Alliances may be established between children in the same family if they feel unthreatened by each other. Greater competition usually exists between adjacent siblings than between alternate siblings. Parents strongly influence their development of lifestyle by encouraging either competition or cooperation among them. For healthy personality development, each child's individuality should be nurtured and respected and comparisons by parents of siblings' characteristics and abililities avoided.

Homework Assignment:

Review carefully the information presented in the study phase of this meeting. Carry out consistently the two childrearing approaches which you have selected based upon knowledge of Erikson's psychosocial stages. Also continue to use the parenting methods you began previously during the study of Gesell's theory. At our next meeting, be prepared to discuss your experiences in using these approaches with your children.

Break: (15 minutes)

Counseling Phase: Session Four

During this fourth session, most group members are ready to work on problems at a deeper, more meaningful level. They begin to examine specific behavioral alternatives for handling difficulties and conflicts with children. For most parent groups, this is the beginning of the working stage of the group. The members and leader continue efforts to gain insights into parents' feelings and behavior and those of children in light of the concepts discussed during the study phases. Group participants generally interact freely at this stage.

The group leader continues to serve as facilitator for some parent interactions while group members assume increasing responsibility for the group. Because relationships and trust are now firmly established, the counselor is likely to begin to use certain counseling techniques to help members look more deeply at their own childrearing behaviors and to examine more fully the factors contributing to their concerns and difficulties. This is part of the essential first step in the decision making process.

The Fifth Meeting

Study Phase

This session focuses upon the continued study of the Adlerian theory of personality development. Mistaken goals of the misbehaving child and Adlerian childrearing approaches are introduced and discussed. In addition, a practice exercise is provided to assist parents to identify and respond constructively to the mistaken goals of misbehaving children. Because completion of this exercise is important, parents should be sure to finish it at home prior to the next session if it is not completed during the group meeting.

Before beginning to study the new material, the group will spend about 15 minutes discussing the homework assignment and reviewing the study content of the previous meeting.

Discussion of Homework Assignment

The homework assignment asked that parents try out the two new childrearing approaches which they had selected based upon Erikson's theory. Also, the parenting approaches begun during the study of Gesell's work were to be continued. Group discussion should provide opportunity for members to report what they have done in using these approaches and what their children's attitudinal and behavioral responses have been.

It is vital that the group provide encouragement to members for continuing efforts to modify their patterns of parenting behaviors in positive ways. Such encouragement is especially necessary for those parents who seem to be making only intermittant rather than consistent use of the new approaches being learned.

Continued support by the group is also important for those who feel somewhat discouraged because benefits seem slow in coming. Understanding of the feelings of these parents should be conveyed to them by the group. When appropriate, they should be assisted to examine their attitudes and behaviors in making these parenting changes and to plan specifically how they will proceed. The group should keep in mind the fact that the childrearing methods presented in this program must be used consistently over a considerable period of time before they become natural, easy to use, and bring about improved parent-child relations.

Review of Adlerian Theory of Personality Development

Briefly review together the study content of the fourth study phase. Be sure to include consideration of the following concepts:
1. the goals of behavior
2. fictional finalisms
3. biased apperception
4. lifestyles
5. family atmosphere
6. family constellation
7. birth order

The Misbehaving Child

Along with the joys of parenthood, there are also many challenges, demands, and frustrations involved in the childrearing role, even for parents whose children tend to be agreeable and cooperative most of the time. To parents of children whose typical behavior may be described as "misbehavior," the parenting role frequently seems overwhelming and discouraging. Their continuous struggles and disagreements in trying to make children behave eventually cause them to feel disheartened about improving the quality of parent-child relationships and family living. They are likely to wonder why these particular children are so "bad" or "willful" and what they themselves are doing that is wrong.

Understanding why children misbehave is essential for breaking the destructive behavior patterns which have been established in such parent-child interactions. Children who misbehave consistently are children who are discouraged and unhappy. In their efforts to achieve a sense of significance, belonging, and competency, they have formed conclusions about themselves and others which have caused them to adopt mistaken goals. They have come to believe that the only way in which they can be important, find their place in the world, and overcome the problems of daily living is by attaining mistaken goals.

The mistaken goals of misbehavior are adopted in a special sequence or pattern by children; as each of these goals, in turn, causes children to experience increasing unhappiness and discouragement, they turn to the succeeding goal. Initially, the goal of misbehavior is undue attention. Continuous and excessive attention is sought by these discouraged, unhappy children through a variety of behaviors. If constructive parenting techniques are not utilized in response to their behaviors, these children become more discouraged and move to the second goal, power.

Continued engagement by children in power struggles with parents leads in time to their adopting the goal of revenge which is the third mistaken goal. If their negative behavior is allowed to continue, these children ultimately move to the final and most destructive goal of misbehavior, inadequacy, helplessness, or withdrawal.

Mistaken Goal One: Bid for Undue Attention

All children need and deserve a reasonable amount of attention and service from their parents. However, discouraged and unhappy children who have adopted undue attention as their goal seem to want these constantly, no matter what is going on. They seek attention and service even when it is not appropriate to the situation or when it may be detrimental to the well-being of other family members. They pursue attention and help at almost any costs and even prefer negative attention rather than none at all.

By being charming and coy or by whining, demanding, or dawdling, they bid for, and generally receive, continuous attention and service from parents. What they really seek is proof that they are important and valued; in truth, they feel neither. Although they constantly seek reassurance that they matter and belong, the reassurance is never lasting. Thus, their behavior continues.

Some examples of typical bids for undue attention or service by children are:

1. Constantly getting mother or father to stop their activities in order to do whatever activity the child wants or to give help with tasks which the child can do independently.
2. Always interrupting adults when guests are present.
3. Generally seeking attention when a parent is talking on the telephone, even if it is only a brief conversation.
4. Typically asking "why?" although the child already knows the answer.

When parents fulfill these bids for undue attention or service, children erroneously conclude that their mistaken methods are indeed the right way to gain a sense of belonging and significance. Furthermore, because their attention-seeking and demanding behaviors do not contribute to their own well-being or that of their parents, children's feelings of discouragement and unhappiness continue to intensify as this destructive pattern of behavior persists.

Mistaken Goal Two: The Struggle for Power

If parents have attempted to use force as a means for stopping them from seeking undue attention or service, children move to the second mistaken goal of misbehavior, the struggle for power. When this happens, they begin to use power to win the battle with their parents. They do this by becoming uncooperative, openly defiant, or quietly obstinate. Too frequently, they refuse to do what is asked of them or to abide by the established rules of home and school. They operate in the belief that they can achieve importance by showing others that they can do what they want to do.

Daily parent-child interactions become power struggles as parents and children try to show each other who is boss. Children resort to trying to seize power because they are unconsciously afraid of being overwhelmed by the stronger power of their parents.

Power struggles can occur over a variety of situations such as doing homework, going to bed on time, putting away toys or other belongings, and even washing hands before meals. The following incident is a typical power struggle:

Each evening mother calls the child to come to the dinner table to join the family. The child continues to play and ignores her request. The mother calls the child several more times, but the child does not come. The mother then repeats her request with the warning of a spanking; still, the child continues to defy her. Finally, mother screams and spanks the child who is then taken to the bedroom.

In this parent-child interaction, each of them has used power to try to control the behavior of the other. Although both are angry and disturbed, the child actually accomplished the goal of exerting power by upsetting the mother and not coming for dinner after all. Sometimes, children reach the point where causing the parent to be upset becomes a powerful source of satisfaction.

However, neither parents nor children ever are real winners in power struggles. These struggles result in severe damage to parent-child relationships and in unpleasant, disruptive family life. If they are allowed to continue, they also cause children to experience deeper, more pervasive feelings of discouragement and unhappiness.

Mistaken Goal Three: The Goal of Revenge

Continued power struggles between children and parents cause children to become even more discouraged and unhappy about themselves. Eventually, they come to think of revenge as the only way to achieve importance. They have reached the conclusion that they are not liked and do not belong but that they can make an impact upon others by hurting them. From their perspective of discouragement, they see themselves as bad, unworthy, and unlikeable.

Acts of revenge by children can take a variety of forms as they attempt to hurt others and to get even in order to receive attention. Some lie, steal, or destroy property. Others hurt and disappoint their parents through hostile actions or words. Some even try to strike back at their parents by physically hurting or taunting more favored or younger children in the family.

Parents' efforts to stop such behavior through the use of force, humiliation, or punishment merely serve to reinforce children's negative beliefs about themselves. In reality, these children are crying out for acceptance, love, and belonging although their behavior engenders anger, frustration, and rejection on the part of their parents.

Mistaken Goal Four: Complete Inadequacy, Helplessness, or Withdrawal

The most dishabilitating and critical of the four goals of misbehavior is the final one—inadequacy, helplessness, or withdrawal. Children adopt this goal after their efforts to gain significance and belonging through undue attention, power, and revenge have not brought them the desired results. They have become completely discouraged and defeated and have given up on themselves. They are convinced of their own worthlessness and feel hopeless about themselves and their lives.

Too often, because their passive, withdrawn behaviors do not place great demands upon parents or continue to seek overwhelming attention, adults fail to recognize the serious nature of their problems. It is advisable for parents to seek professional assistance for children who have reached this stage of discouragement.

Sometimes children's behavior may be influenced concurrently by more than one of these goals. This generally occurs when children are in advanced stages of discouragement. For example, a child might engage in certain behaviors seeking revenge while also indicating some signs of passivity and withdrawal. The four mistaken goals of misbehavior are applicable only to children from birth to age ten. This is the period during which their attention is focused primarily on establishing relationships with parents, family members, and adults who are important to them. Around the age of eleven, when their primary interests turn to peer relationships, disturbing behavior must be viewed from a different perspective.

Childrearing Approaches: Responding to Children's Goals of Misbehavior

Parents can effectively use their knowledge of these mistaken goals for planning how to help misbehaving children to adopt more constructive goals. First, parents must identify the specific mistaken goal or goals which their children have adopted. This can be done quite easily by analyzing how they generally respond to the child's misbehavior. Parents naturally tend to react impulsively when children misbehave and to give children what is being sought according to their mistaken goals. For example, the child seeking undue attention typically receives it from the parents, even if it is in the form of a reprimand.

The best childrearing techniques for helping misbehaving children require that parents not give the results children desire. This causes their children's behavior to become useless. In essence, parents should not respond in ways to help children achieve their mistaken goals. It is important that parents not tell children their conclusions regarding these goals. Revealing these is not helpful in bringing about positive changes and may even be damaging.

Strategies for Responding to Children's Mistaken Goals

1. If children are demanding undue attention or service, do not respond to their tactics. Avoid giving the undue attention or service under any circumstances.
2. If children seek power, do not become involved in a power struggle. Instead, sidestep the issue. If you refuse to become involved in power struggles, their behavior becomes ineffective.
3. For children who want revenge by hurting you, understand their motives and sense of discouragement. Avoid feeling hurt or showing hurt feelings. Do not try to get even with them by using punishment, humiliation, or force.
4. For children who have withdrawn or given up, seek professional assistance to help them discover their abilities and to feel competent. Show love, encouragement, and respect in interacting with them. Parents' attempts to help children who have this extreme mistaken goal to learn to develop a sense of belonging, security, and competency will require consistent effort over a considerable period of time.

Additional Positive Childrearing Approaches

Positive childrearing methods are conducive to the healthy development of all children. For helping children who have developed destructive lifestyles and adopted mistaken goals, much persistence, patience and understanding in utilizing techniques will be required of parents.

1. Acknowledge your children's accomplishments to them. Avoid comparing one child to another and avoid fostering competition among your own children. Each child is unique, and each will have strengths and weaknesses. Remember to build on strengths and to minimize weaknesses.

2. Allow your children to try new experiences. The movement toward independence is a gradual process. The first trip to the store alone and the decision about what to wear to school are important steps toward growing self-responsibility.

3. Allow yourself the right not to be perfect. The process of encouragement is a continuous one—a pervading attitude on your part. If once in a while you fall short, don't give up. Your continued efforts eventually will be fruitful.

4. Use praise carefully so that it does not become the purpose for your children's behavior. A "Thank you for your help" or "You did that all by yourself" is more effective than lavish praise which can lead them to believe that if one is not praised, what one has done is not worthwhile. Remember that children can feel rewarded inside themselves for mastery of skills and tasks accomplished.

The Use of Encouragement

Using encouragement is effective for helping children to develop confidence, competency, and self-respect. Without intending to do so, parents often interact with children in ways which cause them to become discouraged and to lose faith in themselves. By doing things for them which they are capable of accomplishing or by refusing to allow them to assume responsibility, we convey a lack of confidence in them. Frequently, their offers of help are refused, and they are told that they are too young or too small to assist us. Through such acts, we discourage children from being responsible, self-directive, and competent.

Ways to Provide Encouragement

1. Allow your children to assist you in many household tasks when they offer to help.

2. Encourage them to become increasingly active in their own self-care and care of their possessions. If they seem slow at tasks, allow enough time for children to complete them while still maintaining the family schedule.

3. Encourage them to attempt new tasks as they indicate interest and readiness. Avoid saying that things are too hard for them to do. If a task is difficult for them, you may work beside them at the same task to model the appropriate behavior. Baking cookies or fixing the salad can be a satisfying learning experience for child and parent.

4. Allow them to make mistakes. Avoid protecting them from errors or humiliating them when one occurs. Help them to understand that it is okay not to be perfect. (Even mothers and fathers make mistakes.) Use children's mistakes as pleasant opportunities for learning. Acknowledge their disappointment and then provide encouragment for success the next time they try this particular task.

Respect for the Child

Too often respect is viewed from only one aspect in parent-child relations. It is widely accepted that children should show respect for parents. However, little attention is paid to showing respect for children. It is important to think of parent-child relations as requiring mutual respect. Children can learn to respect themselves only if they have been shown respect during their growing up years.

Showing Respect for Your Child

1. Children need regularity and orderliness in their lives. Respect them by providing an orderly, predictable pattern of living—one in which there is regularity and consistency in their lives.

2. Each child is a unique person. Accept children's rights to be persons apart from you, to have their own feelings and attitudes.
3. Each child has abilities and weaknesses. Show respect for your children's ability to cope with many life situations and to make decisions. Encourage them in these endeavors. Allow them to try to solve many of their own problems, even if they occasionally meet with failure. Provide support and understanding as they develop new life concepts and skills.
4. Avoid rearing your children to feel that they are worthwhile only if they live up to your expectations and demands. Encourage them to develop personal goals and interests.
5. Never use humiliation and criticism as a childrearing strategy. These destroy children's feelings of confidence, significance, belonging, and self-respect.
6. Have high, but reasonable expectations for children. These should be established in light of children's developmental stages, abilities, interests, and family lifestyles. They should not be the result of parents' desires to enhance themselves by their children's accomplishments.
7. Take time to listen to your children and to show understanding of their feelings and attitudes. Allow them the right to have feelings and opinions different from yours.
8. Involve your children from their early years in planning, problem solving, and decision making regarding family matters. This can range from participating in family decisions regarding vacations and outings to determining how to maintain a neat household.
9. Have firm and reasonable limits for your children. Showing respect for your children does not mean treating them like adults. We show respect by allowing them to occupy their own unique role as children within the family.

10. Teach them to respect order from their earliest years by firm and calm insistence and by modeling orderliness in the home environment. Children who always leave their possessions in disarray should not be allowed to use them the next time they want them. If children leave their clothing and toys strewn around their room, parents should make it clear that they will not clean the room and that they do not like such disorder. If necessary, close the door so that you do not have to see it. Avoid preaching, warnings, inconsistency, unpleasantness, and hostility in helping your child to acquire a respect for order.

11. Help your children to develop respect for the rights of others. Establish early and maintain consistently fair rules regarding the rights of both parents and children. Communicate these with firmness and calmness to the child.

    For example, if children interfere with the right of their parents to visit quietly with guests in the home, they should be given calmly the choice of stopping the interfering behavior or being taken from the room. The choice is up to the child. If the behavior continues, the child should be taken from the room.

12. Treat all your children with equal respect. Recognize and respect each child's unique qualities. Encourage cooperation rather than competition.

Practice Exercise: Mistaken Goals

This activity is designed to assist parents to identify the mistaken goals of misbehavior and to respond appropriately. Read each situation independently; then the group should answer the following questions about each situation:

1. What is the child's mistaken goal?
2. How might the parent have handled the situation better?

Because of the importance of this exercise, it is strongly recommended that any portion of it which is not completed during this session be done by parents prior to the sixth meeting.

Situation One

Nancy, age six, was playing with her toys on the kitchen floor while mother prepared dinner. "Nancy, in a few minutes it will be time for dinner. Please clean up your toys now so that we may eat in here. Your toys are all around." Nancy continued to play.

In a few moments, Daddy arrived home from work. "Nancy, pick up your toys," he ordered. However, Nancy continued as before.

"Dinner is ready now," said Mother. "If you expect to eat, pick up your toys."

Nancy stood up to come to the table. At this, Mother yelled "Why can't you ever do what you are asked? Sit down at the table now and eat. But remember, after dinner, you will have to pick up your toys."

When dinner was finished, Nancy announced that her favorite television program was on and went to watch it. Mother grabbed her, shook her, and sent her to her room. Nancy screamed, "You pick up the toys, I hate you." Later Mother picked up the toys and put them in Nancy's toy box.

The Fifth Meeting

Situation Two

Dad took Billy shopping with him at the grocery store. As they passed the cookie display, Billy, age five, said "I want some cookies. They look good." "Not today, son," Dad replied. "Aw-c'mon, Dad," Billy whined, following him reluctantly. "Stop being such a baby. We have cookies at home," his father replied.

As Dad continued the shopping, he realized that Billy no longer was with him. After a search, he found Billy playing at the water fountain, squirting water on the floor. Angrily, he said, "Look at you—all wet. Billy, I want you to stay with me. Come on now."

"I'm tired and thirsty," Billy complained, dragging his feet along. Soon they reached the produce display. Billy picked up an apple and started tossing it in the air.

"That does it, Billy, Now you can sit in the cart like a baby. This is the last time I ever take you with me." You're just a big baby."

Developmental Childrearing

Situation Three

Amy, age eight, was kept home from the playground at her mother's angry insistence. Amy's room had been messy for days—strewn with toys and clothing. "I want your room cleaned up now," Mother ordered. Scowling, Amy slowly went to her room.

A half hour later, Mother went to see if Amy had finished putting her things away. She found Amy sitting on the bed playing with her doll. She grabbed the doll away from Amy and slapped her, screaming, "You're supposed to be cleaning up your things."

Amy screamed back, "All you do is yell at me." She ran from the room and out the front door. Mother began to pick up some of the clothes from the floor and put them away.

Situation Four

Jimmy, age nine, played ball outside with his friends after school until dinner time. After dinner, his father demanded, "Is your math homework done yet?" When the boy replied that it was not, his father sternly ordered him to start it immediately and to show the work to him when it was finished. "And I want it done right," Father warned. "I'm tired of your poor math grades."

On the way to his room to begin his homework, Jimmy angrily shoved his six-year-old brother and punched him. At the sound of the younger child's crying, Father came running. "I've told you a hundred times not to hit your brother," he shouted, as he slapped Jimmy. "See how you like being hit by someone bigger than you are."

Weeping, Jimmy yelled at him, "You always take his side. You're just a big bully."

Situation Five

Leslie's mother was expecting company for dinner and was not ready for their arrival. "Leslie, I'm in a hurry. Dust the living room for me and be careful not to break anything in there."

"I can't," protested Leslie, age ten. "I don't know how. I've never done it before."

"Yes, you can. Go ahead. Hurry up," said her mother.

In a few moments, there was the sound of a crash from the living room. Mother found Leslie crying. Broken glass, water, and flowers were spilled on the carpet and the table.

"Why can't you ever do anything right?", her mother demanded. "I should have known better than to depend on you for help."

The Fifth Meeting

Situation Six

Stephen, age six, was playing as his mother read the evening newspaper. It had been a long and difficult day and she was very tired.

"Play with me, Mommy," Stephen begged.

"Not now, Steve," she answered. I'm tired. I played with you for two hours this afternoon. Why don't you look at one of your books? I want to read my newspaper now."

Reluctantly, he began to look at the pictures in a book. In a few minutes, he asked, "Why is the boy laughing in this picture?"

"You know that story. I've read it to you many times. He is laughing because it is his birthday and he is happy."

Stephen turned pages for a few more minutes. Then pushing her newspaper aside, he climbed up in his mother's lap and said, "I love you, Mommy. Let's talk a while."

"I love you too, Stevie. All right. I'll read the paper later."

Discussion of the six situations in this exercise, including identification of the children's mistaken goals and alternative parent responses, may be found in *Appendix A*.

Homework Assignment:

Review thoroughly the study material of this session and complete the practice exercise if it was not finished during this meeting. Also continue to use the childrearing approaches which you have chosen during previous sessions.

Break: (15 minutes)

Counseling Phase: Session Five

The group is well established and is functioning as a cohesive working unit by this fifth session. Although some members may have begun to make tentative decisions regarding childrearing concerns during previous sessions, it is during this one that most parents are ready to make decisions and carry them out.

The process of problem solving and decision making actually was begun during the first counseling session of the group. The essential steps in this process are: 1) identifying the problem; 2) analyzing the problem in order to understand the factors involved; 3) identifying possible approaches for solution; 4) exploring these approaches in terms of their likely effectiveness and feasibility to be carried out; 5) prioritizing these according to effectiveness and feasibility; 6) deciding upon the approach or approaches to be used; 7) carrying out the approach or approaches selected; and 8) assessing the effectiveness of the approach(es) used. If the desired results have not been achieved from this first decision after a reasonable amount of time and effort, the succeeding prioritized choices, in turn, may be carried out. Most group members are at steps five or six in the problem solving process at this time.

In interactions during this session, continued attention should be given to recognizing members' feelings and attitudes and conveying understanding of these as the group explores individual concerns and identifies possible solutions. Keeping in mind the right of each person to determine one's own decisions, it is critical that members avoid imposing advice or forcing decisions upon others in the group. Instead, the group should work to provide support and encouragement for helping members to make their own decisions and to carry them out.

The Sixth Meeting

Study Phase

During this study phase, two additional Adlerian childrearing approaches are presented: the use of natural consequences and the use of logical consequences as methods of discipline. In addition, the use of listening techniques, as advocated by Thomas Gordon, is introduced as a method for improving parent-child relations. A practice exercise is included to help parents to acquire skill in communicating with children.

Before beginning to discuss the new study material, the group should review together the following:

1. the goals of behavior
2. the mistaken goals of misbehavior and why children adopt these goals
3. constructive parent responses to the goals of misbehavior, including the use of encouragement and respect

In addition, the group should discuss any items on the practice exercise which were completed as part of the homework assignment.

Childrearing Techniques for Use in Parent-Child Conflicts

A constructive alternative to using threats and punishment as techniques of discipline is parents' use of natural and logical consequences in conflict situations with children. A natural consequence is action that results from the child's behavior, with no interaction from others. For example, a child who refuses to get up on time in the mornings, despite mother's warnings about being late for school, is allowed to encounter the consequences of this behavior. Mother does not permit herself to be caught up in a power struggle by nagging, punishing, or helping. Instead, the child experiences the results of one's own behavior by having to walk to school rather than riding the school bus and of facing an irate teacher if one arrives late.

The use of natural consequences is appropriate for many conflict situations. The child who continuously gets a parent's attention by always arguing against wearing sweaters or coats when the weather is cold is ignored regarding this. The natural consequence of such behavior is to experience the discomfort of feeling cold once or twice. In using natural consequences, the parent consistently steps aside from conflict with the child about the issue, and the child soon learns to adopt more responsible behavior.

A logical consequence is an action established by parents which is to take place if the child engages in a specific behavior. When parents decide upon the use of a logical consequence as a replacement for existing techniques for dealing with parent-child conflicts, it should be explained to the child in advance and at a time when the offending behavior is not in evidence. The child needs to understand what will happen each time one does the particular thing that has been resulting in conflicts with the parent. In order for this to be an effective childrearing approach, the action selected must be pertinent to the unwanted behavior so that it is seen by the child as a logical and reasonable sequel. And, equally important, the logical consequence must be used consistently whenever the behavior occurs and without anger on the part of parents.

The following are examples of parents' use of logical consequences:

Danny, age nine, generally ignored his parents' repeated calls to come indoors from play to eat dinner. Because they delayed serving until his arrival, the food frequently was dry and cold and both parents were furious with him. Thus the dinner hour often was an unpleasant time. Scoldings such as "How many times do we have to ask you to come when you are called for dinner?" and "You never think about anyone but yourself," resulted in sullen silence from Danny and angry, upset feelings in his parents. Sometimes his father resorted to spanking him, but still this behavior continued.

Danny managed to keep his parents busy with him and also engaged them in a power struggle. He was quite successful in training them to wait for dinner until he was ready to eat. Repeated use of logical consequences could help to alter this continuing destructive pattern of parent-child conflict.

In using logical consequences, Danny's parents tell him briefly, without anger or recrimination, that, hereafter, he will be called only once for dinner because they like to eat on time. He has the choice of eating with them when called or not eating at all— neither dinner nor snacks later during the evening. Whatever he chooses to do about this is acceptable to them. From that time on, his parents proceed to eat their dinner on time and to ignore Danny's late arrival. He is neither provided food, punishment, nor scolding if he fails to appear when called. Although some parents dislike the idea of their child missing a meal, it is obvious that the child's health will not be damaged if a meal is missed occasionally.

The Sixth Meeting

Susan, age seven, continued to leave her books and toys all over the living room although her mother constantly reminded her to pick them up. When Mother could no longer bear the messy condition of the living room, she would threaten Susan with punishment and order her to pick up her belongings, standing over her grimly and watching. Generally, this resulted in angry words from Mother and crying by Susan who would run to her room and slam the door. Then Mother would pick up Susan's possessions and put them in her room so the living room might be neat.

Mother used threats which she did not carry out and took too little constructive action in this conflict. In addition, she ended up giving Susan undue service. Mother needs to take the time to teach Susan quietly and calmly about care for her possessions. In using logical consequences here, Mother calmly informs Susan that any of her belongings left lying in the living room will no longer be available to her. Then, if Susan continues to leave her books and toys in the living room, Mother picks them up and hides them away so that Susan does not have future access to them. The use of logical consequences leaves the choice of action to the child and also allows parents to preserve their own rights and dignity. Furthermore, this technique makes home life more pleasant and agreeable.

Communicating with Children: The Use of Listening Techniques

The nature and quality of parent-child relations are deeply affected by the methods of communication parents use in interactions with children. Because few adults are trained in communication skills, we tend to "talk at" our children and rarely truly listen to what they are saying.

In our interactions with them, we often use such approaches as ordering, lecturing, warning, threatening, and shaming. We are quite likely to respond to their statements to us according to our own perceptions and goals, giving little thought to their feelings and motivations. Interacting with children in these ways does not promote good parent-child relations. In fact, many of these methods block open communication, cause conflict situations, and convey to children a lack of understanding, acceptance, and respect for them. This results in their feeling unimportant, unworthy, and discouraged.

The Sixth Meeting

Many problems in parent-child relations may be solved by parents' consistent use of effective communication techniques. Foremost among these is empathic listening. This technique requires the use of empathy—that is, putting oneself in the child's place when listening to what is being said. It enables us to comprehend the child's feelings as well as the meaning of the words being said.

This kind of listening is necessary in order to be able to respond to children in ways which show understanding and respect. Learning to use empathic listening so that it becomes a natural and integral part of the way we communicate with children takes time, effort, and practice. It is a technique which also necessitates sensitivity and patience. However, because it is such a critical aspect of effective communication and can bring great benefits to our relationships with children, it is well worth the time and attention.

The following practice exercise is designed as a beginning to assist parents to develop the skill of empathic listening. Read each statement carefully. Then decide what the child is feeling and jot down the feeling word for each of these. Because these statements are presented without any related background information, you may find that more than a single feeling seems appropriate for some of the examples. The correct responses to the examples are found at the conclusion of the exercise.

Practice Exercise: Identifying Feelings of Children

1. Child: "I hate my teacher. She sure is crabby. She always yells at everyone."
2. Child: "Everyone picks on me at the playground. They never let me play."
3. Child: "Look at my model plane. I made it all by myself."
4. Child: "I have a test tomorrow. I know I'm going to fail it."
5. Child: "Leave me alone. I don't want to talk to you or anyone else."
6. Child: "You and Dad always think that Charlie does things better than I do—no matter how hard I try."
7. Child: "Only three more days till vacation. Wow."
8. Child: "I guess I shouldn't have hit Nancy but she really made me mad. Do you think she will still be my friend?"
9. Child: "I lost my homework paper. My teacher will scream at me."
10. Child: "You always want me to clean my room. It's my room and I like it the way it is. I wish you would stop nagging me."
11. Child: "Daddy says that I can invite Billy to go to the picnic with us."
12. Child: "Mommy, you promised we could go to the fair and now you say you can't go today. This is the last day it will be here. It won't come again till next year."
13. Child: "You always give him a bigger piece of cake than you give me."
14. Child: "I want to play with them. But they might laugh at me if I miss the ball."

Answers to Practice Exercise: Identifying Feelings of Children

1. The underlying feeling of the child sending the message seems to be anger. If the child's relationship with the teacher has been negative over a period of time, the child's feeling might be discouragement.
2. The most likely feelings for this child are hurt, left out, and sadness.
3. The child feels proud, happy, and a sense of accomplishment.
4. This child is sending a message which conveys worry, fear, inadequacy, and possibly even discouragement.
5. If the statement is not typical of this child, the underlying feelings are anger and hurt. However, if the child makes similar statements frequently, it could indicate discouragement, withdrawal, or hopelessness.
6. This child feels a sense of inadequacy or failure and may well feel discouraged about ever "measuring up" to Charlie.
7. This child is feeling excited, happy, and great anticipation.
8. This child's underlying feeling is regret as well as some concern regarding the future of the relationship with Nancy.
9. This child's message conveys fear, dread, worry, or anxiety.
10. The underlying feeling in this message is anger.
11. This child feels excited, happy, and pleased.
12. This child is obviously disappointed and perhaps even angry.
13. Envy or jealousy are the probable feelings of this child.
14. The underlying feelings here are fear, anxiety, and inadequacy.

Homework Assignment:
1. Identify one continuing issue of conflict between you and your child. Select a natural or logical consequence appropriate to the child's developmental stage and the nature of the conflict. Whenever that conflict issue arises, consistently use the natural or logical consequence you have chosen. Be prepared to report on this to the group next week.
2. Listen for your children's feelings when they talk with you. Select a particular interaction that you have during this week with your child. Record in writing what each of you said during this interaction and the feelings underlying your child's statements. Bring these to the next meeting of the group for purposes of discussion.

Break: (15 minutes)

Counseling Phase: Session Six

Members continue to work on modifying their childrearing approaches, incorporating into their decision making parenting techniques and understandings about child development acquired during the study phases. Some members report to the group the experiences they have had in carrying out childrearing decisions made during previous sessions. These are discussed and analyzed in terms of such factors as children's reactions to the new strategies, members' feelings in utilizing them, and the successes and difficulties encountered.

Feedback is provided regarding possible ways to improve these efforts and other methods which might be more effective. Based on this, further decisions often are made by members. Decisions regarding childrearing should be stated clearly in terms which describe the specific behaviors members will use in interacting with their children.

The group climate is one of unity, acceptance, empathy, and openness. In many ways, a strong sense of "family" is evident. The leader generally is much less active in fostering interactions among members as they themselves assume increasing responsibility for the work of the group.

Role playing is an especially helpful method for giving members the opportunity to practice at this time the new parenting approaches which they have decided to try at home. The group can provide additional benefits to members by critiquing their practice efforts and making suggestions for improvement.

The Seventh Meeting

Study Phase

The first part of this study phase is used for a review of the use of natural and logical consequences in parent-child conflict and the technique of empathic listening. Opportunity will be provided for members to report their experiences in using natural or logical consequences with their children as was assigned at the last meeting. Discussion of the successes and diffulties resulting from the use of these methods and planning for continued efforts are important. Following this, parents will share the written recordings of their interactions with children, including identifying feelings, which were also part of the homework assignment.

In this study phase, the communication skill, responding to children's feelings, is introduced and practiced by members through the use of role playing. Also presented is the self-statement technique for parents to employ for expressing their own feelings in parent-child interactions. These are adapted from Thomas Gordon's technique of "I" messages.

Responding

When we have become aware of our children's feelings through the use of empathic listening, we are ready to respond to them more effectively. This can be accomplished by using an empathic response which 1) indicates understanding of the feelings and 2) recognizes the reasons for those feelings. First, let us look at a typical parent-child interaction.

Billy, age eight, has lost his new wallet in school today. He had received it as a gift from his grandmother yesterday and had been delighted with it. When he arrived home from school this afternoon, he announced to his mother, "I lost my new wallet in school."

Mother answered, "I told you not to take it to school with you. Why can't you ever hang on to your things? If you had listened to me, this never would have happened."

Billy ran to his room crying.

Analyze this parent-child interaction by answering the following questions:

1. Were mother's comments constructive and appropriate to the situation? If so, why? If not, why not?
2. How was Billy feeling when he first came home and announced that he had lost his wallet?
3. How did Billy feel as a result of her comments?

Discussion:

Analysis of this parent-child interaction reveals that this mother's comments were harmful and inappropriate. She scolded, accused, and lectured him, implying that he was incompetent and useless. Also she was using this situation to punish Billy for disobeying her order not to take the wallet to school. (A natural consequence of his taking it to school is for him to do without it.) She went beyond the present situation and made a larger accusation of incompetency by asking why he could not "ever hang on to his things." When Billy first came home and announced that he had lost his wallet, he was angry at himself and disappointed and upset about the loss. As a result of his mother's statements, it is likely that he also then felt discouraged, hurt, incompetent, misunderstood, and worthless.

Let us look at the same situation with Mother responding quite differently to Billy's loss of the wallet.

Billy, age eight, has lost his new wallet in school today. He had received it as a gift from his grandmother yesterday and had been delighted with it. When he arrived home, he announced to his mother, "I lost my new wallet in school."

Mother answered, "You really are mad at yourself and disappointed about losing your new wallet."

Billy replied, "I sure am. It was my first wallet. I should have taken better care of it. I hope someone finds it and turns it in at the lost-and-found desk tomorrow."

Billy nodded in agreement and went to his room.

Analyze this parent-child interaction by answering the following questions:

1. Were Mother's comments constructive and appropriate to the situation? If so, why? If no, why not?
2. How was Billy feeling when he first came home and announced that he had lost his wallet?
3. How did he feel as a result of her comments?

Discussion:

Analysis of the second parent-child interaction suggests that mother's remarks were both constructive for Bill and appropriate to the situation. She conveyed to him through her responses an understanding of his feelings and recognition of his reasons for those feelings.

Her responses enabled Billy to communicate openly to her his feelings of regret and his hope that the wallet would be found. She also acknowledged to him understanding of this hope to get the wallet back. Although Billy continued to regret the incident, his mother's statements helped him to feel understood, respected, and worthwhile.

This responding technique of communicating to the child understanding of feelings and the reason for them can greatly improve parent-child relations. It conveys respect for and acceptance of the child's feelings, allowing self-respect and the right to be a unique individual. Sometimes, in our efforts to be good parents, we deprive children of this right by ignoring, minimizing, denying, or ridiculing how they feel.

The following is an example of a parent denying a child's feelings although he is trying to help the child.

Joan, age seven, refused the neighborhood children's invitation to join them outside to play kickball. Instead, she sat looking out the window at their game. When her father asked her why she had not joined them, she said, "I'm not good at kicking the ball. I always miss the kick, and everyone laughs at me."

Her father said, "Don't be so silly. You're as good at it as anyone else."

Joan's father was denying her feelings of inadequacy at kickball and the fear of embarrassment if her friends were to laugh at her. A better response to her statement is: "You feel afraid to play because you might miss the ball and get laughed at." Father then might even offer to help her acquire this skill. This type of response is known as empathic responding.

We can respond to our children's feelings more constructively by sending back such messages which acknowledge both their feelings and their reasons for feeling as they do. The following format is a pattern of an empathic response which incorporates both of these components: "You feel (feeling word) because (reason why child feels that way)."

Practice Exercise: Role Play Using Empathic Responding Technique (15-20 minutes)

The group should utilize the practice *Identifying Feelings of Children* from *Study Phase Six* for role playing the technique of empathic responding. All group members should be involved in this activity; members should take turns assuming the roles of parent and child for each of the situations. Those who assume parent roles should follow the pattern for this type of response as described in the study phase of this session. The group should provide feedback to each of the role play vignettes regarding the responses used and how they might be modified for more effective communication with children.

Communicating Parent Needs for Respect and Understanding

Parents, as well as children, have needs and rights of their own in family living. Some parents tend to disregard to a large entent their own needs and rights, believing that they are doing what is best for their children. However, for healthy child development, it is essential that parents and children treat each other with respect and consideration. The child who is permitted to be inconsiderate, self-centered, and disrespectful of the needs of parents is acquiring a destructive lifestyle characterized by a lack of concern for and interest in fellow human beings. When this occurs, parents often feel hurt, angry, hostile, and resentful toward their children and wonder what went wrong.

Respect for parents as well as for children can be developed by parents' establishing and maintaining reasonable, firm limits which preserve the rights of both parties. In addition, parents need to express their own feelings to children as a means of gaining respect, understanding, and cooperation.

The general format for empathic responses to show parents' understanding of children's feelings can be adapted to express parents' feelings to children. The following example demonstrates the use of this format for purposes of conveying parents' feelings and the reason for those feelings:

Parent Self-Statement: I feel (parent's feeling) because (reason for parent's feeling).

Example: I feel angry because there are toys all over the living room when I am expecting company.

This approach can be a helpful mode of communication in parent-child interactions. It should be used calmly and assertively rather than angrily or in a confronting manner.

The following situations serve to demonstrate parents' use of self-statements:

1. Typical Parenting Response: Billy, age nine, had developed the habit of staying out-of-doors playing with his friends long after dark each evening. Every time he came in late, his father lectured him about the dangers of being out after dark, concluding with, "You never think about anyone except yourself." Despite these angry confrontations, Billy continued to stay out after dark.

   Self-Statement Communicating Parent Feelings: "Billy, I always feel worried when you stay out to play after dark. It seems unfair that my feelings about this are not considered."

2. Typical Parenting Response: Nancy, seven years old, kept interrupting her mother who was trying to rest. Finally, Mother yelled at her, "Find something else to do and stay out of my room. Can't you ever leave me alone?"

   Self-Statement Communicating Parent Feelings: "I am very tired and need to rest now. I feel angry because my rest is being disturbed. I will call you when I have finished resting."

If the first self-statement does not have the desired effect, another statement should be made which has stronger and clearer feelings and intent. If Nancy had ignored her mother's first self-statement regarding the need for uninterrupted rest, her mother might follow up with this kind of intensified statement, "I don't like being ignored. I feel furious when you pay no attention to my feelings. I am exhausted and need some rest."

Such follow-up statements also must be delivered as calmly and unthreateningly as possible. This can be accompanied by a message showing understanding of the child's feeling, such as, "You wish I would spend some time with you now, but I am very tired." Usually these approaches are effective. However, if the parents' rights still are ignored, it is time to take action. In this case, Nancy should be given the choice of leaving the room or being taken from the room. The use of logical or nature consequences is appropriate at times when this sequence of self-statements does not produce the desired outcome.

Homework Assignment:

Practice at home this week the use of empathic listening, empathic responding, and self-statements in interacting with your children. Be ready to report to the group at the next meeting your experiences in using these techniques. Also review the study material presented during this session.

Break: (15 minutes)

Counseling Phase: Session Seven

Group members continue to discuss their experiences and feelings in carrying out at home the decisions they have made in the group. Where appropriate, further problem solving continues. Members interact freeling and respond openly to each other. Deeper self-insights continue to be developed as the group members explore their behaviors and feelings regarding efforts to modify childrearing methods and establish better parent-child relations. In their interactions, they provide each other with positive feedback for improvements noted and also furnish support and encouragement for trying alternative approaches when desired goals are not met.

As the self-esteem and understanding of group members increase, they assume greater and more effective leadership for the group during the sessions. Although this enables the group leader to be generally less active in facilitating the work of the group, the leader continues to provide direction and support when they are needed. At the close of this counseling session, the leader reminds the group that only one more session remains. Group members must begin to prepare themselves for coping with the impending loss of the closeness, understanding, acceptance, and support they have been receiving from the group.

The Eighth Meeting

Study Phase

This last study phase begins with a session for members to report their experiences in using the listening and responding techniques and self-statements in communicating with their children. The group should assist members to analyze their usage of these techniques and to make changes if needed. Role playing of actual parent-child interactions, as reported by members, may be employed here to help strengthen the skills and confidence of those who had difficulty in using these techniques correctly with their children.

In the new study material, an Adlerian approach to family problem solving is introduced. Following this, a summary is presented of Burton White's and Jean Watt's findings (1973) regarding effective childrearing practices.

Family Problem Solving

All families experience some difficulties in daily living for which solutions must be found. An effective, democratic approach to family problem solving is the family council. This is a weekly meeting of all family members in which the following occurs: 1) problems and concerns are discussed calmly, 2) possible solutions to these problems are identified, and 3) a solution is selected by majority opinion. The solution chosen is carried out during the forthcoming week and is evaluated at the next meeting of the family council. Once the decision has been made, the issue cannot be discussed again until the following meeting when another solution may be sought if the previous one has proved to be ineffective.

This approach to family problem solving has the advantage of involving all family members in sharing responsibility for making decisions and implementing solutions. The following are guidelines for the family council:

1. The family council meets each week at the same hour of the same day. The time for a meeting is not changed without the agreement of all family members.
2. All members of the family are expected to be present. If anyone is absent from a meeting, that person must adhere to whatever decisions are made at the meeting.
3. All family members have the right to bring up problems. Decisions regarding problems are made by the group—not by the parents—and are decided by majority opinion. Each person in the group has equal status, and everyone has the right to be heard.
4. Leadership for the meeting is rotated to include all family members, even the younger children unless they are tots. The chairperson conducts the meeting so that respect and democratic principles are maintained.
5. All family members are expected to abide by decisions made at these meetings.
6. Issues of concern may be brought up again at the next council meeting if any members are dissatisfied with a previous decision. The emphasis in meetings should be upon action to be taken rather than upon blame for the problem.

Here is an example of problem solving in a family council meeting:

Jimmy, age ten, has been experiencing much frustration and anger because his three younger brothers are careless with his toys and belongings when he is not at home. They leave them scattered in various parts of the house and sometimes break them. This has resulted in many fights among the brothers and also has caused much unpleasantness in the family. Jimmy has brought this issue before the family council and has asked, "What are we going to do about it?"

Various solutions are suggested by the boys and their parents. One of the younger boys suggests that they be allowed to play with Jimmy's toys if they put them back. Father recommends that the younger children stay out of Jimmy's room unless they have his permission to enter. Another child suggests that Jimmy put the toys he is willing to share with them on the bottom shelf of his bookcase and that they not touch any of his other toys or belongings. Jimmy recommends that only his eight-year old brother be allowed to use his things and that the younger ones should not.

The group, by majority opinion, decides that Jimmy should put any toys he is willing to share on the bottom shelf of the bookcase and that his brothers not use any of his other possessions. The decision is carried out and the problem, in this instance, is solved. If it had not worked well, the problem could have been reintroduced at the next or a subsequent meeting.

All members are heard; all participate in the process of problem solving and decision-making. Because of this active participation, all family members are more likely to carry out the solution than if the parents impose their own decisions upon the children. Parents who have tried this approach to family problem solving report that it is highly effective when used consistently as described.

The Eighth Meeting

Effective Childrearing Practices: White and Watts

Over a period of years, Burton L. White and his associates at Harvard University studied the development of competency in young children. In doing this, they identified those childrearing practices which promote the optimal development of competency in children. The following childrearing recommendations are taken from a book by Burton White and Jean Watts entitled *Experience and Environment, Volume I* (pp. 242-243) which is an outcome of their extensive studies. To assist children to become competent and responsible persons, parents should:

1. Talk with children extensively on levels they can understand.

2. Furnish children with accessibility to many objects and a wide range of experiences and people.

3. Assist children to feel that what they are doing is interesting and important.

4. Lead children to believe that they can expect help and encouragement most of the time, but not all of the time. If the time that help is requested is not convenient, parents should say so.

5. Show and explain things to your children, mostly on their initiative, but sometimes on your own. Explain how things work and why certain things occur as they do.

6. Provide firm and consistent rules and limits. Feel secure enough to say "no" to certain activities or requests without worrying that your children will not love you.

7. Be imaginative with your children by making interesting suggestions and associations.

8. Encourage your children's natural inner desire to learn.

9. Help your children to acquire the idea that doing tasks well and completing them is desirable.

10. Make your children feel secure by providing love and affection and an orderly, predictable environment.

Facts About Effective Parents

White and Watts found that effective parents served as teachers on the "go." They did not spend the majority of their time with their children, but they were responsive to their children's interests. These parents were usually affectionate, permissive rather than authoritarian, and indulgent with their children. However, they were able to take a stand on issues consistently and firmly. They explained reasons to their children for rules and limits, listened to their children's feelings and views regarding these, and still maintained their position unwaveringly. They usually, but not always, responded to their children's requests for help immediately and with enthusiasm. If the time was inconvenient, they were able to state this so that their children did not always receive immediate attention.

Effective parents encouraged their children's desire to learn and communicated freely with them. Most of them had positive attitudes toward life in general, were considerate and attentive, and enjoyed their children at whatever ages they happened to be. They allowed their children freedom to experience new situations and interests and permitted them to take some risks in terms of safety, exerting caution rather than being overprotective. They were not concerned about being meticulous housekeepers, but instead maintained homes in which furniture and objects were functional rather than "for show." These parents helped their children to acquire positive attitudes toward doing tasks well and completing them. It is interesting to note that family size and income were not factors affecting competent childrearing.

Break: (15 minutes)

Counseling Phase: Session Eight

In this final group counseling session, members tend to show less openness and intimacy than during the previous few sessions, as if ready for departure. This is the typical way in which we prepare ourselves for functioning without the support of the group. Some members may request additional group sessions, seeking to prolong this experience. The group leader must deny any such requests due to the demands of time and the nature of this program. Through considerable study, it has been determined that the experiences provided in the eight meetings of this program are adequate for helping parents to improve certain parenting attitudes, better understand child behaviors, and acquire more effective childrearing methods.

Because of the close relationships which are generally established in parent groups, some groups have found it enjoyable to meet informally with the leader for luncheon or coffee at a time several weeks after the final group meeting. During these informal get-togethers, parents have the opportunity to share with each other the outcomes they observe from continuing the childrearing efforts which were begun during their participation in the program.

In most instances, the group leader will be available after the end of the program for individual counseling sessions with members who request them. If they are interested, parents who have participated in this program should indicate to the group leader their desire to participate in future parent groups.

During this last session, members should be assisted by the group to identify individually the progress they have made in chidrearing and to specify the ways in which they shall continue their efforts after the conclusion of the group. As a final activity, members should assist the leader to evaluate their experiences in the *Developmental Childrearing* program and also should feel free to make recommendations to help the leader successfully conduct future groups.

A Message to Parents

Your participation in the *Developmental Childrearing* program has provided you with a variety of experiences to help you achieve greater understanding of yourself as a parent—your feelings, attitudes, and typical approaches to raising children. Along with this, you have gained deeper insight into child development and childrearing techniques which parents can employ to help their children to proceed successfully through the developmental stages. Throughout the program, you have worked to improve your parenting methods, and, based upon your increased knowledge and skills, you have made positive changes in practices and attitudes. Many of you already have seen some benefits from your efforts.

Changing our childrearing methods and attitudes is difficult even while we are members of a group from which we receive encouragement, support and recognition for what we are attempting to do. Continuing our efforts when we no longer have the support of the group is even more demanding. And yet, it is vital to continue what has been begun in this program. We, as parents, are our children's most important teachers. From their interactions with us, they develop the attitudes, beliefs, and behaviors with which they will live their lives.

There are some things that parents can do after the group has ended to help themselves maintain what they have started in the group. One approach is to reward oneself for continued efforts to improve the quality of parenting. Giving oneself a psychological pat on the back when it is deserved can provide needed encouragement. Another helpful approach is to keep a daily record of the positive childrearing approaches used. Seeing in writing the improvements being made furnishes a tangible accounting of our efforts. A daily checklist or diary entry is suitable for this purpose.

It is advisable to encourage your spouse to employ the same constructive childrearing approaches which you are now using. This applies also to other adults such as grandparents or babysitters who spend considerable time with your children. Discuss with these adults what you are doing and why. It may be helpful for them to read pertinent sections from the study phases of this program. Where possible, urge your spouse to participate in a *Developmental Childrearing* group so that both parents are compatible in their approaches to childrearing.

Positive changes in your relations with your children are likely to appear gradually rather than all at once. Probably there will be times when you feel discouraged and wonder if your efforts will ever be successful. As has been stated many times during the program content, consistent use of these parenting practices over a period of weeks or even months is necessary for achieving lasting benefits. Therefore, please be patient with yourself and with your children as you seek to carry out the important work you have begun in this childrearing program.

Appendix A

Discussion of Practice Exercise: Mistaken Goals

Situation One: Nancy, age six.

Mistaken Goal: The mistaken goal in this case is power. Mother allowed herself to be engaged in a power struggle with Nancy.

A more positive approach would be for Mother and Daddy to tell Nancy calmly that she cannot come to the table until her toys are picked up. They should begin to eat without her and should continue their meal completely and without recriminations if the toys are not yet picked up. Nancy should not be served dinner nor be allowed to eat snacks if she does not come to the table while dinner is still in progress. If the toys are still lying around when dinner is finished, Mother should take them calmly and hide them away so they will not be accessible to the child.

Situation Two: Billy, age five

Mistaken Goal: Billy's motive is undue attention. He has managed to keep Father busy with him through misbehavior. Father should clearly establish in advance with Billy the rules for shopping trips and then firmly and calmly enforce them. Humiliation should not be used to control Bill's behavior. A positive approach toward helping Billy feel worthwhile is to give him some responsibility for getting the shopping done. If the disturbing behavior continues, Billy should be removed from the store and taken home.

Situation Three: Amy, age eight

Amy's motive is power. She and her mother are engaged in a power struggle to show each other who is boss. This power contest is making life miserable for both of them. Children can be very adept at holding their own in power struggles. Mother has the right not to enter the room for cleaning up or any other purpose till Amy gets it done. The door can be kept shut at all times so it does not disturb Mother to see the messy room. Amy will have to live with her own disorder.

Situation Four: Jimmy, age nine

Mistaken Goal: Jimmy sought revenge against his father by picking on his brother. Feeling discouraged and worthless, this was his way of striking back. Father reacted to his act of revenge as the boy had expected he would, thus continuing the destructive cycle of behavior.

A more democratic parenting approach is needed here. Jimmy needs encouragement, understanding, and respect in his efforts to master arithmetic rather than accusations of failure and threats of punishment. A private, quiet discussion between parent and child to provide encouragement and support for the child's efforts is more appropriate. This prevents Jimmy from feeling the need to seek revenge by hitting his brother. It also can help him feel more confident about accomplishing his math assignment. By hitting Jimmy when he hurt his brother, Father gave him another reason to seek revenge in the future.

Situation Five: Leslie, age ten

Mistaken Goal: Leslie's mistaken goal was helplessness and withdrawal. She has given up on herself. Leslie needs to have consistent opportunities and responsibilities to participate in household tasks. This requires repeated training by Mother so that Leslie can experience some success. Mother should use encouragement. If failures occur, they should be the basis for future training and learning in order to give Leslie a sense of competency. If improvement in the relationship is not observed within a reasonable time, profesional assistance should be obtained.

Situation Six: Stephen, age six

Mistaken Goal: Stephen's mistaken goal was undue attention. Stephen was demanding constant attention by being sweet and charming. He felt that he did not belong unless he kept his mother constantly busy with him.

Mother should not give in to his bid for undue attention, no matter how charming Stephen may be. She should continue her reading. Stephen needs to develop feelings of belonging through more constructive behavior. Mother should make every effort to notice him when he is being self-sufficient and cooperative in the family situation so that he feels significance and belonging at these times.

Developmental Childrearing

References

Dreikurs, R., & Stoltz, V. *Children the Challenge.* New York: Hawthorn Books, 1964.

Erikson, E.H. *Childhood and Society.* New York: W.W. Norton, 1963.

Gordon, T. *Parent Effectiveness Training.* New York: Peter H. Wyden, 1970.

Ilg, F., & Ames, L. *Child Behavior from Birth to Ten.* New York: Harper & Row, 1955.

White, B., & Watts, J. *Experience and Environment: Major Influences on the Development of the Young Child.* Englewood Cliffs, NJ: Prentice-Hall, 1973.